New Jersey ❓ What Exit ❓

300 Questions and Answers
About People, Places, and Events
in the Garden State

Gerald Tomlinson

Lake Hopatcong, New Jersey

For information, write:

> Home Run Press
> 19 Harbor Drive
> Lake Hopatcong, NJ 07849

If a copy of this book is not available at your local bookstore, you may order one by sending $15.00 to the address above. The book will be shipped postpaid. New Jersey residents add 6% sales tax.

Library of Congress Catalog Card Number: 95-95079   CIP

The information in this book is obtained from sources believed to be reliable, and every effort has been made to be as accurate as possible. However, some of the information herein is subject to change, and the author and publisher make no representation that this book is free from error.

Cover: Tom Kinter
Cartoons: Matt Tomlinson
Photographs: Gerald Tomlinson

Printed in the United States of America

ISBN 0-917125-05-3

Preface

There's more to New Jersey than the New Jersey Turnpike.
There's even more to it than the Garden State Parkway.

Small, prosperous, and picturesque, the state has been getting a
better press recently. Not great, but better.

Even people in New York City (at least some of them) are
beginning to recognize that New Jersey is an actual place and not
just a one-liner. Consider. Where do the football Giants and Jets
play? Where are Ellis Island and the Statue of Liberty?

Pennsylvanians, too, know in their hearts that *something* exists on
the eastern side of the Delaware River.

In fact, New Jersey is a marvelous little state, and we should all
be proud of it. We should know something about it as well.

Do we? What better way to find out than through a quiz?
So saying, here's the quiz. And not just one quiz either, but a
small assortment of quizzes. To wit:

☞ *The Basic Quiz.* One hundred not-too-difficult questions.

✿ *The Super Quiz.* One hundred more demanding questions.

Bonus Puzzlers. Sixteen topical quizzes with weighted-score
answers. You can combine these quizzes however you
wish.

The Photo Quiz. Five questions whose answers can be
found on page 60 (nonreaders of prefaces could lose
out: this is the only reference to them).

The Back-of-the-Book Quiz. Nine questions that may inspire
the curious to examine the book. Or may not, as the
case may be. Answers are page 35.

Grab a pencil! Break the curve!

Acknowledgments

By its nature, this book draws on a wide array of sources. First among them is *The New Jersey Book of Lists*, for which I thank my co-author Ronald A. Mayer. Two other books that proved invaluable were John T. Cunningham's *This Is New Jersey*, 4th ed., and Barbara Westergaard's *New Jersey: A Guide to the State*. Several recent Rutgers University Press books were helpful, among them Marc Mappen's *Jerseyana: The Underside of New Jersey History*, Peter Genovese's *Roadside New Jersey*, Janice Kohl Sarapin's *Old Burial Grounds of New Jersey: A Guide*, and the reissued classic, *The WPA Guide to 1930s New Jersey*. There are two useful trivia quizzes in print about the Garden State, and I would have been remiss to ignore them: The New Jersey Historical Society's *Jersey Jeopardy*, 2nd, ed., and Albert and Shirley Menendez's *New Jersey Trivia*. Two periodicals that are always informative on New Jersey people, places, and events are *New Jersey Monthly* and *The Star-Ledger*. Of particular help were Mark Di Ionno's many *Star-Ledger* features on New Jersey lore and byways. Several questions in the book were suggested by Matt Tomlinson, Kristin Smith, and Will Lai. Ideas for questions or statements resulted from Bob Burnett's courses at County College of Morris and clippings provided by Herman A. Estrin. Some came from correspondence following publication of *The New Jersey Book of Lists*, for which I thank Jeanne Boyle, Jeff Wayne, Norman J. "Footlocker" Sandler, Jeanne Van Dorn Mauk, and Robert A. Erlandson. Most of the other information was obtained at or through the Morris County Free Library in Whippany or the Jefferson Township Public Library. Finally, thanks to Alexis, who suggested doing this kind of book, to Matt, who reshaped and enlivened the manuscript version, and to Eli, without whom the book would lack a cover.

Contents

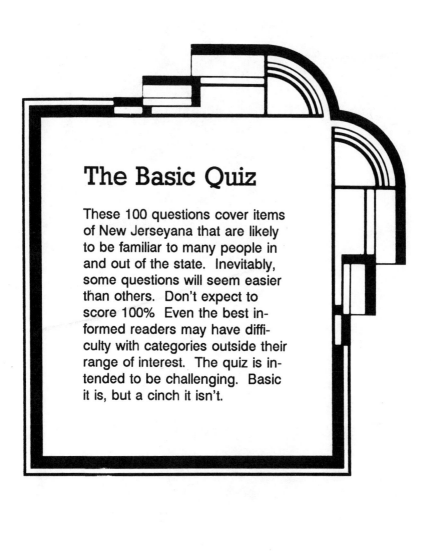

The Basic Quiz

These 100 questions cover items of New Jerseyana that are likely to be familiar to many people in and out of the state. Inevitably, some questions will seem easier than others. Don't expect to score 100% Even the best informed readers may have difficulty with categories outside their range of interest. The quiz is intended to be challenging. Basic it is, but a cinch it isn't.

Minor league baseball returned to New Jersey in 1994. This is a scene at Skylands Park, Frankford Township, home of the New Jersey Cardinals. A question about the other new minor league team, the Trenton Thunder, is on page 20.

Entertainers

Many actors, actresses, singers, and musicians have been born in New Jersey or have made the Garden State their home. These ten questions focus on some of the best known Jersey-born entertainers.

1. Comedy straight man Bud Abbott was born in Asbury Park. His sidekick, eleven years younger, was born in Paterson.

   ☞ 1 Who was Bud Abbott's partner in comedy—the chubby fellow who kept asking, "Who's on first?"

2. This Princeton-born singer and actor played the title role in Eugene O'Neill's *The Emperor Jones* and sang "Ol' Man River" in Jerome Kern's *Show Boat.*

   ☞ 2 Who is this famous New Jerseyan whose bass voice embraced both folk songs and Shakespeare?

3. Born in Hoboken, "Ol' Blue Eyes" first gained fame as a pop singer in the bobby-sox era. As an actor, he won an Oscar for his role in *From Here to Eternity.*

   ☞ 3 Who is this great performer who made it to the top "My Way," in the words of his signature song?

4. She debuted in the film *On the Waterfront*, winning an Academy Award as Best Supporting Actress and followed with a fine performance in *A Hatful of Rain.*

   ☞ 4 Who is this blonde star, born in Newark, who played opposite Cary Grant in *North by Northwest?*

5. Concetta Franconero attended Belleville High School and achieved early popularity in *Where the Boys Are*—the movie as well as the hit song.

☞**5** Under what stage name did Concetta Franconero act and record her best-selling singles of the 1950s?

6. He appeared in several films in the '50s and '60s before attracting widespread notice. He hit his stride with *Easy Rider* in 1969.

☞**6** Who is this Neptune-born superstar who went on to win plaudits in *Chinatown, One Flew Over the Cuckoo's Nest, Terms of Endearment,* and *Batman?*

7. They call him "The Boss," and no wonder. A native of Freehold, this hugely popular singer and songwriter titled his first album *Greetings from Asbury Park, N.J.*

☞**7** Who is this Grammy, Oscar, and Golden Globe winner whose "Born in the USA," "Jersey Girl," and "Streets of Philadelphia" are known worldwide?

8. An accomplished actress, she was born in Summit and grew up in Bernardsville. She has won Oscars twice and praise for virtually every performance.

☞**8** Who is this ex-cheerleader at Bernards High School who earned Academy Award nominations for her roles in *Silkwood* and *Out of Africa?*

9. He received a recording contract that specified how he would henceforth spell his name. The minor name change became the title of his first album in 1984.

☞ **9** Who is this rock star from Sayreville who won a Golden Globe Award in 1991 for the song "Blaze of Glory"?

10. Her early success as a model was eclipsed by her later renown as a singer. A Newark-born superstar, she won a Grammy in 1993 for "I Will Always Love You."

☞ **10** Who is this talented performer who appeared opposite Kevin Costner in the film *The Bodyguard,* playing—of all things—a rock star?

BONUS PUZZLERS / 1

The Face Is Familiar

a. What actor from East Orange won an Oscar for Best Supporting Actor in 1939 for his role in *Stagecoach?* (5 points)

b. What Newark-born actress starred as Adelaide in both the stage and screen versions of *Guys and Dolls?* (3 points)

c. What actor from Orange played the harried Amity cop in the film *Jaws?* (3 points)

d. What Elberon-born actor made his film debut in *Lost Boundaries* in 1949? (5 points)

e. What character actor from Jersey City appeared in the films *Working Girl* and *Silence of the Lambs?* (4 points)

[20-point total—answers on page 40]

Movers and Shakers

A number of important men and women in American history have a close connection with New Jersey. Some were born here. Others came here to teach, study, experiment, or serve. These ten questions deal with such notables.

1. This world-famous inventor was born in Ohio, but his laboratories at Menlo Park and West Orange link him inextricably to New Jersey.

   ☞ **11** Who is this Jersey-based man who perfected the phonograph and countless other inventions?

2. The founder of the American Red Cross settled in Bordentown in 1851 and a year later established a one-room free public school there.

   ☞ **12** Who is this woman who during the American Civil War was called the "Angel of the Battlefield"?

3. Just one President of the United States was born in New Jersey—specifically in Caldwell. He is the only President elected to two nonconsecutive terms.

   ☞ **13** Who is this New Jersey native who was elected governor of New York and President of the U.S.?

4. Born in Elizabeth, he was a salty U.S. naval officer called "Bull" by the press in World War II. His leadership helped secure Allied victory in the Pacific.

   ☞ **14** Who is this admiral whose forces won the Battle of Leyte Gulf?

5. When she was elected in 1993 as New Jersey's 60th governor, she became the first woman in that office.

☞ **15** Who is the governor, born in New York City, who broke the gender barrier in the Garden State?

6. Although born in Staunton, Virginia, he rose to power in New Jersey, first as president of Princeton University, then as governor of the state.

☞ **16** Who is this Democrat who ran for President in 1912 and who, as President, fought futilely for U.S. membership in the League of Nations?

7. Mrs. Mary Hays is known to history by a different name. At the Battle of Monmouth in the Revolution, she carried water to the Colonial troops.

☞ **17** What name did the soldiers give to Mrs. Hays, a Freehold resident, for her acts of mercy on the sun-baked field of battle?

8. He is perhaps the best-known scientist of modern times. An emigré from Nazi Germany, he continued his landmark work in physics on the Princeton campus.

☞ **18** Who is this Nobel-winning physicist who wrote the letter to President Franklin D. Roosevelt that prompted research leading to the atomic bomb?

9. This astronaut graduated from Montclair High School, flew combat missions in Korea, and became the second man to walk on the moon.

☞ **19** Who is the astronaut, nicknamed "Buzz," whose moonwalk followed that of Neil Armstrong?

10. A precocious graduate of Rutgers University, this 1976 Nobel Prize winner in economics taught at the University of Chicago starting in 1946.

☞ **20** A famed monetary expert, he was born in Brooklyn and raised in Rahway. He argued for laissez-faire economic policies. Who is he?

BONUS PUZZLERS / 2

Front-Page Obits

a. What President of the United States died in Elberon on September 19, 1881, after being shot in Washington, D.C.? (5 points)

b. What businessman, founder of a department store chain and long associated with R. H. Macy, died in South Orange on May 11, 1944? (3 points)

c. What young woman, comatose for years, was taken off life support, lived for some time, but finally died on June 11, 1985, in Morris Plains? (4 points)

d. What Civil War general and legendary (but not actual) inventor of baseball died in Mendham on January 16, 1893. (3 points)

e. What young woman, murdered in Hoboken in 1841, inspired Edgar Allan Poe to write "The Mystery of Marie Rogêt"? (5 points)

[20-point total—answers on page 40]

Events

New Jersey has had its share of headline-making events over the years. A few of them have been happy occurrences, but, as with major news stories in general, many have involved crimes, disasters, and other unpleasantries.

1. Alexander Hamilton, one of the founders of Paterson—not to mention the nation—died on July 12, 1804, of a gunshot wound suffered in a duel the day before.

   ☞ 21 Who fired the fatal shot at Alexander Hamilton on a grassy shelf above the Hudson at Weehawken?

2. One of the worst disasters in New Jersey history occurred on the night of September 8, 1934, when a cruise ship caught fire off Sea Girt.

   ☞ 22 What is the name of this ill-fated ship on which 134 people perished?

3. A bitter defeat for organized labor occurred in Paterson in 1913. The Industrial Workers of the World (IWW) went on strike to protest increased work demands.

   ☞ 23 What industry was being struck by these workers whose union base was the Botto house in Haledon?

4. In June 1967 the administration building at Glassboro State College (now Rowan College) became internationally famous because of a three-day meeting.

   ☞ 24 Who were the two heads of state who met at Glassboro in 1967 to try for a thaw in the Cold War?

5. Few crimes have caught the attention of the American public so completely as the kidnapping of a baby boy from his parents' home in Hopewell.

☞ **25** Who was the infant taken from an upstairs bedroom at the Highfields estate on March 1, 1932?

6. It was the world's largest and most fashionable lighter-than-air craft. As it approached its mooring mast at the Lakehurst Naval Air Station, it burst into flames.

☞ **26** What was the name of this German dirigible whose disastrous end on May 6, 1937, was vividly described on radio and spectacularly photographed?

7. New Jersey's canal boom lasted only briefly, but it produced two major canals. One was the Delaware and Raritan Canal, sections of which still exist.

☞ **27** What was New Jersey's other famous canal, the one from Phillipsburg to Newark, that opened in 1831 and extended to the Hudson River in 1836?

8. There is a famous painting by Emanuel Leutze titled *Washington Crossing the Delaware*. The event it shows occurred on Christmas night, 1776.

☞ **28** The next morning Washington's troops attacked the Hessians in one of the decisive battles of the Revolution. What is the battle called?

9. Canals and railroads were vital means of transportation in the nineteenth century. Then in 1903 came the Wright Brothers with their flying machine.

☞ **29** Newark Airport, the state's busiest, opened in 1928. The state's second busiest airport, home of an aviation museum, opened in 1920. What is it?

10. A radio broadcast in 1938 threw Americans into panic. The Martians were coming! They were landing near a tiny community "22 miles from Trenton"!

☞ **30** What dot on a road map of New Jersey—hardly a town at all—did 23-year-old Orson Welles identify as the site at which space aliens were arriving?

BONUS PUZZLERS / 3

Dateline New Jersey

a. On September 7, 1921, what well-publicized annual event occurred in Atlantic City for the first time? (3 points)

b. On November 9, 1971, what pious accountant murdered his mother, his wife, and his four children in their home in Westfield? (4 points)

c. On October 26, 1918, what disease—a scourge that killed millions of people in a worldwide epidemic—claimed 76 lives in Newark? (3 points)

d. On July 19, 1954, what ex-Governor of New Jersey was charged with 38 forgeries committed while he was in office? (5 points)

e. On February 26, 1959, what noted New Jersey mob boss committed suicide (according to the official finding) at his mansion in West Orange? (5 points)

[20-point total—answers on page 40]

Buildings

Historic buildings abound in the Garden State. Nearly every community has its own. Certain of these buildings have significance and appeal beyond the towns and cities in which they stand, including the ones in these ten questions.

1. The Morristown National Historical Park, established in 1933, was the federal government's first historical park. A gleaming white mansion is its centerpiece.

   ☞ **31** What is the name of the Morristown home in which General George Washington spent the winter of 1779-80?

2. A poet's house in Camden is now designated a State Historic Site. It was once the home of the man who wrote *Leaves of Grass*.

   ☞ **32** This great American poet is buried in Harleigh Cemetery, Camden. What is his house called?

3. This military building, dating from the mid-1750s, once housed (at various times) British troops, Hessian troops, Continental troops, and prisoners of war.

   ☞ **33** What is the name of this building in Trenton, now a museum, that is the last of five orginal units?

4. The local historical society maintains this 1879 church as a historical museum, and no wonder. As St. James Chapel it was attended by seven U.S. Presidents.

   ☞ **34** The Church of the Presidents stands on Ocean Avenue in what New Jersey shore city?

5. Richard Stockton, a signer of the Declaration of
   Independence, had this home in Princeton built for
   him in the mid-1750s.

   ☞ **35** What is the name of this house that served for
   many years as the governor's mansion?

6. Although casinos have been profitable in Atlantic City,
   not all of them have survived under their original
   names. The Playboy, for example, is gone.

   ☞ **36** What was the name of the first casino hotel to
   open in Atlantic City—and enjoy nearly a one-year
   monopoly in the gambling trade?

7. One of the most frequently photographed sights in the
   Garden State is a lighthouse reached by crossing
   the Manahawkin Bay Bridge.

   ☞ **37** What is the name of this lighthouse designed by
   General George Gordon Meade, the Union commander at Gettysburg?

8. On a college campus in West Long Branch stands an
   elegant 130-room mansion, once called Shadow
   Lawn, now called Woodrow Wilson Hall.

   ☞ **38** What college owns this impressive abode, the
   home of Daddy Warbucks, played by Albert Finney,
   in the 1982 film *Annie?*

9. New Jersey has diners everywhere, making it hard to
   single out one for special notice. Route 3 West
   from the Lincoln Tunnel features two popular ones.

☞**39** Name either of the two principal 24-hour diners that greet motorists outbound from New York City on Route 3.

10. Two adjoining houses are the birthplaces of naval hero James Lawrence in 1781 and author James Fenimore Cooper in 1789.

☞**40** In what New Jersey city on the Delaware River are these adjacent historic houses?

BONUS PUZZLERS / 4

Within These Walls

a. What is the name of the large animal-shaped building in Margate, built in 1881, a National Historic Landmark that was once a hotel? (3 points)

b. What public library, the site of Vealtown Tavern in the Revolution, is noted for harboring the ghost of a woman who loved a hanged British spy? (4 points)

c. What is the name of the minor league baseball stadium opened in 1994 that is home to the Trenton Thunder of the Eastern League? (5 points)

d. What is the New Jersey high school that gained fame because its principal, flamboyant Joe Clark, wielded a baseball bat to maintain discipline? (5 points)

e. What kind of building in Jersey City came to national attention in 1993 because of Omar Abdel-Rahman's ties to the World Trade Center bombing? (3 points)

[20-point total—answers on page 40]

Businesses

Change is the norm in American business. Several of the nation's largest corporations are headquartered here. But some of the great enterprises of yesterday, such as the Singer Sewing Machine plant in Elizabeth, are gone.

1. Two enterprises dominate the economy of New Brunswick. One is Rutgers University. The other is the company that makes Band-Aids and Tylenol.

   ☞ 41 What is the name of this health-care company founded in 1886 on the banks of the Raritan?

2. A great but defunct automobile company was head-quartered in Trenton. It manufactured the classic 70-mph Type 35 Raceabout of 1911.

   ☞ 42 The company and its cars were named for Trenton's county. What county—and car—is it?

3. A factory at 105 Hudson Street, Jersey City, has a 50-foot clock that faces Manhattan. Its minute hand weighs more than a ton.

   ☞ 43 What New York-based company owns and operates this enormous clock?

4. Andy Warhol did not make this Camden soup company famous, but he did make himself famous in part by painting a picture of its red-and-white cans.

   ☞ 44 What is the name of this company, the world's largest maker of canned soups?

5. Brewing was once a booming business in New Jersey. One prosperous Newark brewer built a fine mansion in 1885 that is now part of the Newark Museum.

☞45 This brewer, like many others, named his beer after himself. What did he call it?

6. The research unit of the American Telephone and Telegraph Company (AT&T) has employed a dazzling array of Nobel Prize winners in physics, including John Bardeen and Arno A. Penzias.

☞46 What is the name of this world-famous AT&T research unit whose scientists at Murray Hill have helped change the ways in which we communicate?

7. This glitzy business got its start in New Jersey, particularly Fort Lee, and then moved to southern California for the sunshine.

☞47 Mary Pickford, Theda Bara, and D. W. Griffith are among those who helped the industry grow in the early 1900s. What is the industry?

8. By far the largest New Jersey representative of the aerospace and defense industry is headquartered in Morristown. The company also makes auto parts.

☞48 What is this corporate giant whose earnings outpace those of most of New Jersey's prosperous pharmaceutical companies?

9. The Rock of Gibraltar, in an insurance sense, is located not in the Mediterranean but in a 24-story building near Newark's Penn Station.

☞ **49** What is the name of this insurance company, the nation's largest, that started in a Broad Street storefront?

10. One of the largest pharmaceutical companies in the United States has long been active in Rahway. It is a leading maker of prescription drugs.

☞ **50** What is this multinational corporation, founded in 1891, whose common stock in 1993 was the most actively traded on the New York Stock Exchange?

BONUS PUZZLERS / 5

Wealth from the Earth

a. What metal, a component of brass, was once mined extensively in the area of Franklin and Ogdensburg in Sussex County? (3 points)   ʒɪɲc

b. What metallic ore, abundant also in Morris County, makes some of the rivers in the Pine Barrens run red? (3 points)   ιɾoɲ

c. What town southwest of Mount Holly is named for the woody natural resource that the region formerly produced in abundance? (5 points)

d. What radioactive metal was discovered in Jefferson Township in the 1970s and might have been mined except for the residents' opposition? (4 points)

e. What mineral, rounded and polished by the action of water, is collected on the beach and sold in gift shops as "Cape May Diamonds"? (5 points)

[20-point total—answers on page 72]   quartz

Places

The Garden State is small geographically, 47th among the 50 states in total area. It outranks only Rhode Island, Delaware, and Connecticut. Yet New Jersey's diversity has caused it be called "America in Miniature."

1. In the late 1600s what is now New Jersey was divided into two parts by a line extending from Little Egg Harbor to a point near the Delaware Water Gap.

   ☞ **51** The capital of West New Jersey was Burlington. What was the capital of East New Jersey?

2. For many decades Essex County was the most populous county in the state. But in the 1990 U.S. Census, Bergen County took over as number one.

   ☞ **52** Newark is the county seat of Essex County. What is the county seat of Bergen County?

3. This Monmouth County town at the mouth of the Navesink River was once the largest manufacturer of military and Boy Scout uniforms in the world.

   ☞ **53** What is this town whose best-known landmark today is probably the Count Basie Theatre?

4. Three of the 21 counties in New Jersey have fewer than 100,000 people each. The least populous county in the state numbered 65,294 people in 1990.

   ☞ **54** What is this sparsely settled county whose county seat is noted for its magnificent 500-year old oak tree?

5. One of the Union's most highly regarded infantry com-
manders in the Civil War was killed at Chantilly,
Virginia, in 1862.

☞ 55 What Hudson County city is named after this
dashing, one-armed major general?

6. Several New Jersey communities began as sites of
Methodist camp meetings. One of the best known is
in Monmouth County near Asbury Park.

☞ 56 What is this town, now part of Neptune Township, that until recently banned Sunday automobile
traffic, boating, bicycle riding, and swimming?

7. If you drive the length of New Jersey on any highway,
north to south (or vice versa), there is one
south-central county you are sure to pass through.

☞ 57 What is this sprawling New Jersey county that
stretches across the state from the Atlantic Ocean
to the Delaware River?

8. Before 1834 this suburban town went by the name of
Bottle Hill. For decades it was known, too, as the
"Rose City."

☞ 58 What is this town, now prosaically named after
an early President, that is home to Drew University
and one of the campuses of Fairleigh Dickinson?

9. Utopian communities come and go. One that came and
stayed is this town founded at the time of FDR's New
Deal. It was first called Jersey Homesteads.

☞ **59** What is the present name (honoring the ex-President) of this one-time communal farm-and factory project that became something of an artists' colony?

10. Liberty State Park, opened in 1976, offers a spectacular view of the New York City skyline as well as ferry service to Ellis Island and the Statue of Liberty.

☞ **60** In what major Hudson County city is Liberty State Park?

BONUS PUZZLERS / 6

Clinton—Named for Bill?

Name a New Jersey town that has the same name as each of the following. (2 points each)

a. a planet
b. the ancient rival of Athens
c. "Mad Anthony"
d. the 20th President of the United States
e. its courthouse
f. a Greek letter
g. the President's home on Pennsylvania Avenue
h. what follows a shuffle in cards
i. the cervix of a young horse
j. the name of a British prime minister

[20-point total—answers on page 72]

Religion and Education

What's this? Mixing religion and education? That's right. After all, Princeton University was founded to train Presbyterian ministers. Religion and education have often been intertwined, as a few of these ten questions indicate.

1. Chartered as Queens College in 1766, in response to a petition from leaders in the Dutch Reformed Church, it is now The State University of New Jersey.

    ☞ **61** What is the name of this university where Nobel Prize winner Selman Waksman studied and taught?

2. One of the premier engineering schools in the nation is located on Castle Point in Hoboken. Its Davidson Laboratory is a world-famous hydrodynamic facility.

    ☞ **62** What is this college that in 1985 annoyed many by granting an honorary degree to Frank Sinatra?

3. Quakers settled West Jersey, and their meeting houses dot the region. This Burlington County town is home to an outstanding Friends School, founded in 1785.

    ☞ **63** What is the town in which this school (only three percent of whose students are Quakers) is located?

4. Newark has many impressive churches, none more awe-inspiring than the one east of Branch Brook Park modeled on the Gothic cathedral at Rheims, France.

    ☞ **64** What is the name of this huge Gothic Revival church that took 55 years to complete?

5. The "best" public high school in New Jersey is hard to determine. Mountain Lakes? Princeton? Tenafly? Maybe, but three of the best are in south Jersey.

☞ **65** Name any of three Camden County high schools that consistently place high in statewide rankings.

6. New Jersey's only Ivy League university ranks among the finest in the nation. Its faculty and graduates make up a virtual *Who's Who* of American notables.

☞ **66** The resident writers have included such literary giants as Eugene O'Neill, John O'Hara, and Joyce Carol Oates. What university is it?

7. George Schultz, former U.S. Secretary of Labor, Treasury, and State, graduated from this private day school in Bergen County.

☞ **67** From what exclusive school with a hyphenated name, located in Englewood, did George Schultz (not to mention Brooke Shields) graduate?

8. The Newark public school system, once highly praised, has had its problems in recent years. But two of its high schools send a high percentage of their students on to college.

☞ **68** Name either of the two Newark public high schools whose percentage of college-bound graduates is right up there with, say, Millburn's.

9. Generally regarded as New Jersey's most famous church, this magnificent house of worship on Broad Street, Newark, dates back to 1791.

☞ **69** What is the name (or nickname) of this Presbyterian landmark?

10. Often thought of as a preparatory school for Princeton, this nearby private boarding and day school, founded in 1810, has a 500-acre campus.

☞ **70** What is the name of this school where Thornton Wilder was teaching when he wrote *The Bridge of San Luis Rey?*

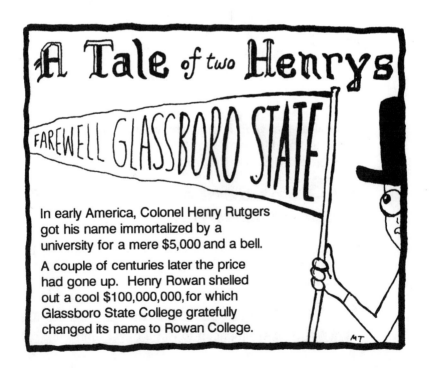

Sports

Many star athletes have been born in New Jersey or have played here. Although the Meadowlands Sports Complex, begun in the 1970s, has attracted New York City teams and millions of fans, these questions deal with earlier events.

1. Arnold Cream, born in Merchantville, became the heavyweight boxing champion of the world in 1951 by knocking out Ezzard Charles.

   ☞ **71** Under what better-known name did this boxing champ from southern New Jersey fight?

2. The first match game in baseball was played in Hoboken on October 21, 1845, between the New York Base Ball Club and the Brooklyn Base Ball Club.

   ☞ **72** This historic baseball game was played in a park overlooking the Hudson. What was the park called?

3. A basketball star at Princeton and later for the New York Knicks, this Missouri-born Rhodes scholar went on to become a U.S. Senator from New Jersey.

   ☞ **73** Who is this politician about whom John McPhee wrote the book *A Sense of Where You Are?*

4. Her great years on the tennis court were 1957 and 1958 when she won the U.S. singles championship and also won at Wimbledon.

   ☞ **74** Who is this East Orange woman who became the first African American to win a major tennis title?

5. A native of Columbia, Alabama, this star athlete moved to New Jersey as a child and won 16 varsity letters at Orange High School.

☞ **75** He played baseball for the Newark Eagles, Jersey City Giants, and New York Giants. Who is he?

6. The first heavyweight boxing championship match to attract a million-dollar gate was fought in 1921 between Jack Dempsey and Georges Carpentier.

☞ **76** In what New Jersey city did this highly publicized boxing match take place?

7. After coaching football at St. Cecilia's High School in Englewood, he gained fame as head coach of the New York Giants and Green Bay Packers in the 1950s and '60s.

☞ **77** Who is this great football coach who reputedly said, "Winning isn't everything—it's the only thing"?

8. Roosevelt Stadium in Jersey City saw many exciting baseball games, but none more electrifying than the one on April 18, 1946.

☞ **78** What historic event did fans witness on that day when a young player for the minor-league Montreal Royals took the field?

9. This track-and-field star graduated from Plainfield High School in 1952 and that summer won a silver medal in the decathlon at the Olympics in Helsinki, Finland.

☞ **79** Who is this athlete who went to the Olympics in Melbourne, Australia, in 1956 and broke the Olympic decathlon record by 50 points to win a gold medal?

10. Many baseball experts consider this the best minor league team of all time. It included such stars as Charlie Keller, Joe Gordon, and George McQuinn.

☞ **80** In what year and in what New Jersey city did this group of future major league stars win the International League championship by 25½ games?

BONUS PUZZLERS / 7

Teams Past and Present

a. Football star Herschel Walker got his pro start playing for what New Jersey team? (5 points)

b. Leon Day was one of the great pitchers in baseball's old Negro Leagues. For what black New Jersey pro team did he play? (4 points)

c. Goalie Martin Brodeur help lead what New Jersey team to the National Hockey League's Stanley Cup in 1995? (3 points)

d. For what New Jersey college team did basketball star Bobby Hurley play before signing on with the Sacramento Kings of the NBA? (3 points)

e. First baseman Mickey Vernon spent 20 years in the majors. Prior to that, for what pro baseball team in New Jersey did he play? (5 points)

[20-point total—answers on page 72]

Superlatives

It's great to be first, best, tallest, largest. Sometimes, with diminutive New Jersey, it's a matter of being a big fish in a small pond. But not always. A few of these superlatives go beyond the borders of the state.

1. According to the 1990 U.S. Census, the second and third most populous cities in New Jersey are Jersey City and Paterson.

   ☞ **81** Which cities in the state are first and fourth in population?

2. There are a number of tall buildings in New Jersey, though none to compare with New York's World Trade Center or Philadelphia's One Liberty Place.

   ☞ **82** How many of the state's three tallest buildings are located in Jersey City?

3. The first young woman from New Jersey to be crowned Miss America was Hackettstown's Bette Cooper in 1937, representing Bertrand Island.

   ☞ **83** Who is the woman from Mays Landing who was crowned in 1984, replacing Vanessa Williams?

4. New Jersey has been a leader in highway design. The state introduced the cloverleaf in 1929 and the center divider called the "Jersey barrier" in 1949.

   ☞ **84** What innovation in highway design appeared first in Camden County way back in 1925?

5. When it comes to the height of its mountains, no one will mistake New Jersey for Colorado. But naturally there has to be a highest point in the state.

☞ **85** The state's highest point is in Sussex County, where a state park is named for it. What is the park?

6. The world's first boardwalk was built in 1870 on the Jersey shore. Many similar boardwalks exist in the state's seaside towns today.

☞ **86** The world's first boardwalk was built by a man with the appropriate name of Alex Boardman. In what town was (and is) it?

7. Atlantic City's old resort hotels, except for the Claridge, were quickly replaced by casino hotels after the advent of legalized gambling.

☞ **87** Which casino hotel has the most rooms—1,624 at last count?

8. Northwest New Jersey has a lake region. Few of the lakes are very large, but the biggest one has a shoreline of more than 40 miles.

☞ **88** What is this large lake with a name that few people from out of state can pronounce?

9. The tiny municipality with the highest per-capita income in New Jersey is in the extreme northeast corner of the state.

☞ **89** What is this wealthy Bergen County community located just off Exit 2 on the Palisades Parkway?

10. Here's a sports first: On November 6, 1869, two football teams met in New Jersey to play the first intercollegiate football game in the United States.

☞ **90** One of the teams that played—the losing team—represented Princeton. What was the winning football team, also from the Garden State, that participated in this historic contest?

BONUS PUZZLERS / 8
We're Number One!

a. What New Jersey community was the first in the United States to be fully lit by electricity? (4 points)

b. The first successful submarine in the world was built by John P. Holland in what New Jersey city? (4 points)

c. An aquifer is an underground source of water. New Jersey has an aquifer with 30 times the full capacity of all the reservoirs in New York City's water system. Where is it? (3 points)

d. In 1642 the first brewery in the United States was established in what New Jersey city? (4 points)

e. What New Jersey state park has the longest system in the nation of cross-country skiing trails covered by artificial snow? (5 points)

[20-point total—answers on page 72]

ANSWERS TO THE BACK-OF-THE-BOOK QUIZ

1. Gold (Sutter's Mill, 1848) **2.** *Akron* **3.** H. Norman Schwarzkopf
4. Thomas A. Edison **5.** Belva Plain **6.** Highlands **7.** Camden
8. Sergeantsville **9.** Six Flags Great Adventure

The Arts

With its well-educated and relatively well-off population, it's not surprising that New Jersey has produced and supported some noteworthy artists, actors, writers, and musicians. The ten questions that follow suggest a few of them.

1. One of America's finest writers attended Princeton University and then penned his first novel about a young man with experiences much like his own.

    ☞**91** Published in 1920, *This Side of Paradise* made its author an overnight success. Who is the author?

2. In his younger days, actor Marlon Brando was one of America's notable leading men. One of his best movie roles was as a misfit in *On the Waterfront.*

    ☞**92** In what New Jersey city was this searing 1954 look at labor strife on the docks filmed?

3. New Jersey has many fine architects. Among the most distinguished is this man, based in Princeton, who is a world-famous exponent of the postmodernist syle.

    ☞**93** Who is this architect, whose projects include the Swan and Dolphin Hotels in Walt Disney World?

4. The cartoonist who introduced the Republican elephant and the Democratic donkey, not to mention the modern image of Santa Claus, lived in Morristown.

    ☞**94** His vitriolic caricatures helped bring down the Boss Tweed ring in New York City. Who is he?

5. Pearl White, known as "queen of the silent serials," showed her stunt-woman training in this well-known early film series produced in 1914.

☞ **95** What is the name of the movie (really a series of episodes) that imperiled Pearl on the Palisades?

6. This New Jersey writer for adolescents has a large and enthusiastic following.

☞ **96** Who is the Elizabeth-born author who wrote, among many other books, *Then Again, Maybe I Won't*, a novel for teenagers set in Jersey City?

7. A pediatrician in Rutherford, his lifelong home, this doctor achieved international fame as a poet, writing in a style he called *objectivism*.

☞ **97** Who is this well-known poet, a Pulitzer Prize winner, who wrote the five-volume, structureless poem *Paterson* about the nearby New Jersey city?

8. You can't mistake his sculptures for anyone else's. Consisting of white plaster human figures, they show ordinary men and women in everyday situations.

☞ **98** Who is this South Brunswick-based sculptor whose Kent State memorial (atypically cast in bronze) stands on the Princeton campus?

9. Born in Newark and raised in Asbury Park, this writer earned a permanent place in American literature with his Civil War novel *The Red Badge of Courage*.

☞ **99** Who is this renowned novelist who died at the age of 28, having already achieved immortality?

10. This theater is housed in a modern building in Millburn. Its original home was in a converted mill that burned down in 1980.

☞ **100** What is the name of this 1,200-seat theater on Brookside Drive that puts on plays and musicals, often with Broadway stars?

BONUS PUZZLERS / 9

A Few Forgettable Films

a. Troma, a low-budget filmmaking company, released a series of movies with a character billed as "the first superhero from New Jersey." What is his name? (5 points)

b. In what movie does Gene Hackman, as Lex Luthor, try to blow up New Jersey? (3 points)

c. This 1980 horror movie was filmed in Blairstown. It spawned eight sequels and a TV show. What is this film, which had Betsy Palmer (and a young Kevin Bacon) in its cast? (3 points)

d. In 1994 the nation was treated to a movie about carjacking in New Jersey. What is the title of this box-office bomb? (5 points)

e. Vernon Township hosted Sterling Hayden and several other stars for this 1978 film, about which New York *Times* critic Vincent Canby quipped, "The gypsies should sue." What is the film's title? (4 points)

[20-point total—answers on page 127]

Photo Quiz—1. New Jersey has several buildings shaped like windmills, but the structure shown here is the real thing. Now operating as a museum, it is the Volendam Windmill in Hunterdon County. What township is it in?

Answers to Bonus Puzzlers 1 to 4

1 / THE FACE IS FAMILIAR **a.** Thomas Mitchell **b.** Vivian Blaine **c.** Roy Scheider **d.** Mel Ferrer **e.** Philip Bosco

2 / FRONT-PAGE OBITS **a.** James A. Garfield **b.** Louis Bamberger **c.** Karen Ann Quinlan **d.** Abner Doubleday **e.** Mary Cecilia Rogers

3 / DATELINE NEW JERSEY **a.** Miss America Pageant **b.** John List **c.** influenza **d.** Harold G. Hoffman **e.** Abner (Longy) Zwillman

4 / WITHIN THESE WALLS **a.** Lucy the elephant **b.** Bernardsville Public Library **c.** Mercer County Stadium (or Waterfront Park) **d.** Eastside High School, Paterson **e.** a mosque

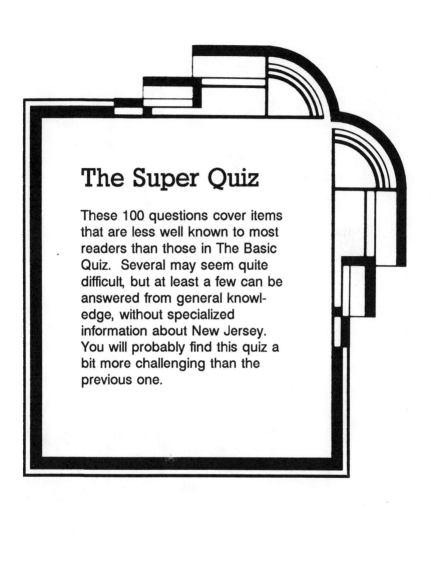

The Super Quiz

These 100 questions cover items
that are less well known to most
readers than those in The Basic
Quiz. Several may seem quite
difficult, but at least a few can be
answered from general knowl-
edge, without specialized
information about New Jersey.
You will probably find this quiz a
bit more challenging than the
previous one.

Photo Quiz 2. The Jersey shore is noted for its boardwalks. Some of them are longer than others, or wider, or offer more rides, amusements, and arcades. The boardwalk shown here is one of the great ones. Where is it?

Entertainers

The performing stars of one era can become the forgotten figures of the next. And in every era there are lesser-known entertainers whose faces are familiar but whose names may escape you. Test your memory with these ten questions.

1. This actor from Montclair once said, "I started at the top and worked my way down." One of his best starring roles was in the 1950 version of *The Asphalt Jungle*.

   ☼1 He played a crazed general in *Dr. Strangelove* and called his autobiography *Wanderer*. Who is he?

2. Her first name was Phoebe, her last name was Mozee, but she had two names in between by which she was known. She was also called "Little Sure Shot."

   ☼2 Who was this expert shooter who lived in Nutley while working for Buffalo Bill?

3. So far this Newark-born actor's most visible role was in a 1990 movie in which he plays Henry Hill, an ambitious young mobster who turns informant.

   ☼3 Who is this star of *GoodFellas*, a film in which another Newark native, Joe Pesci, won an Oscar?

4. Susan Abigail Tomaling grew up in Edison, cleaned apartments while attending Catholic University of America, and debuted in the 1970 film *Joe*.

   ☼4 What name appears in the credits for this talented actress, a co-star in *Thelma & Louise*?

5. A jazz pianist and bandleader, he rose to fame in the 1930s as a major figure in the swing era of jazz. He was known by a nickname suggesting nobility.

☼5 Who is this native of Red Bank, born in 1904, who played piano for silent films at the Palace Theater?

6. Here's a tough one. This protégée of Lola Montez first gained fame in the mining camps of California, then returned east to star in *The Old Curiosity Shop*.

☼6 A 19th-century actress and comedienne, she lived in Mount Arlington when not traveling. Who is she?

7. This famous composer of musicals wrote "Smoke Gets in Your Eyes" for his great Broadway hit *Roberta*, first produced in 1933.

☼7 Who is this 1902 graduate of Newark High School who wrote the music for many stage successes and, later, the scores for several films?

8. This petite character actress, born in Morristown, won an Academy Award for Best Supporting Actress in the first film in which she appeared.

☼8 Who is this woman who played a man in her award-winning performance in *The Year of Living Dangerously?*

9. Francis Castelluccio, a native of Newark, was the lead singer of The Four Seasons, though under a shorter name. One of his recordings is titled "Over Barnegat Bridge and Bay."

☼9 What is the stage name of this singer who had a number-one hit in 1978 with his single of the theme song for the film *Grease?*

10. A gospel and pop singer, she hails from East Orange, where, like many other African-American stars, she got her start in a chuch choir.

☼10 Who is this durable singer whose recordings include "Alfie," "Do You Know the Way to San Jose?" and "What the World Needs Now"?

BONUS PUZZLERS / 10

From Jersey to Stardom

a. Who is the noted film actor, born in New Brunswick, who won an Oscar for his performance in *Wall Street?* (3 points)

b. What is the stage name of this rap artist, born Tracy Morrow in Newark, whose performance in "Back on the Block" won a 1990 Grammy? (5 points)

c. Who is this actor, a native of South Orange, who taught math in Zimbabwe before landing a part on TV's *Melrose Place?* (5 points)

d. Who is this short-statured actor from Neptune who starred in the TV series *Taxi* after appearing in the film *One Flew Over the Cuckoo's Nest?* (3 points)

e. What is the Dickensian-sounding name of this magician, born in Metuchen, who, among his other feats, has levitated a Ferrari? (4 points)

[20-point total—answers on page 127]

Movers and Shakers

Not everyone of importance is a world-famous celebrity. Some of New Jersey's movers and shakers have received media attention and some have not. These ten questions concern people less well known than, say, Yogi Berra.

1. A prominent New Jersey politician, he never served as governor, but he was elected Vice President of the United States in 1896.

   ☼11 Who is this man, William McKinley's veep, who was born in Long Branch and died in office in 1899?

2. She was co-owner and eventually director of one of the best teams in the Negro National League. Imagine her pique when the majors hired away her stars.

   ☼12 What was the name of this woman who was the first to sign Larry Doby and Don Newcombe?

3. Nominated by President Reagan, this associate justice soon became the most consistently conservative member of the U.S. Supreme Court.

   ☼13 Who is this outspoken Trenton-born judge who has voted to overturn many liberal precedents?

4. Born Henrietta Howland Robinson, she was called "The Witch of Wall Street" and in 1916 left an estate valued at $100 million.

   ☼14 What was the married (and familiar) name of this notorious but wealthy miser who lived in Hoboken?

5. For much of the state's history, a governor could not be elected to successive terms. However, several governors served two nonconsecutive terms.

☼15 Only one New Jersey governor has served three nonconsecutive terms. Who is he?

6. One of New Jersey's most popular Congresswomen was a pipe-smoking Republican who lost a close Senate race to Frank Lautenberg in 1982.

☼16 Who is this well-known Congresswoman who represented the affluent 5th District from 1975 to 1982?

7. This Newark inventor developed the process for making patent leather, devised a machine to make nails, and created another machine to shape hats.

☼17 Never a good businessman, he died poor while working on a method for growing giant strawberries. Who is this long-time Newark resident whose statue stands in the city's Washington Park?

8. It is said that only one colonial town in the nation was established by a woman. Located in Camden County, the town is a prosperous suburb of Philadelphia.

☼18 What is the name of the woman who founded this community on the main road from Burlington to Salem?

9. In the days of big-city political machines, the one in Jersey City wielded tremendous power and gained a national reputation.

☼19 What machine politician, born and entrenched in Jersey City, is noted for saying, "I am the law. . . "?

10. The "wagonmaker to the world" based his business in Burlington, offered some 200 models at the height of his success, and built 10,000 wagons a year.

☼20 Who is this entrepreneur who, in addition to his domestic production, built jinrickshas for the Asian market?

BONUS PUZZLERS / 11

Who's the Governor?

a. Who is the New Jersey governor whose two terms, 1947-54, produced a badly needed new state constitution as well as the New Jersey Turnpike? (5 points)

b. Which governor, born at sea, is now honored by having New Jersey's third largest city named after him? (3 points)

c. Which New Jersey governor served two nonconsecutive terms, the first during World War I, the second during World War II? (6 points)

d. Which governor has the distinction of being the son of the state's most famous inventor? (3 points)

e. Who is the New Jersey governor often chided because he had the arena at the Meadowlands Sports Complex named after him? (3 points)

[20-point total—answers on page 127]

Events

Some news stories are quickly forgotten, but others—a very few—become part of the national consciousness. The events on these pages had a life beyond the evening news. See if some, or all, of the ten questions ring a bell.

1. The 1922 Hall-Mills murder case was called the "crime of the century"—but only for a decade or so. The victims were a minister and his choir-singer mistress.

   ☼21 Their bodies were found in Franklin Township, but both were residents of what New Jersey city?

2. In upstate New York someone placed a crude wooden marker over his grave. It read: "Here lies Sam Patch, Such is Fame."

   ☼22 Fame? What was Sam's feat in Paterson on September 30, 1827, that first brought him notice?

3. Clara Maass died in Cuba at the age of 25. A nurse from East Orange, she had volunteered for risky immunization experiments.

   ☼23 What kind of epidemic, then sweeping Cuba, caused Clara Maass to volunteer her services?

4. In 1918 a number of street names in Newark were changed. A new name, Long Valley, had recently been given to a community in western New Jersey.

   ☼24 What was happening that caused people to change the names of their streets and towns?

5. Joseph Francis of Toms River invented a device to rescue people from wrecked ships. In 1850 he helped saved 201 people from the sinking Scottish brig *Ayrshire*.

☼**25** What was the basic principle of Francis's life car that worked so effectively that day off Manasquan?

6. Everyone knows about the Boston Tea Party, a defining moment in our nation's move toward independence. Far fewer know about New Jersey's tea party.

☼**26** In what New Jersey community did men dressed as Indians burn a British cargo of tea in 1774?

7. Arthur Flegenheimer was very big in the Bronx beer trade. But it was at the Palace Chop House in Newark that Flegenheimer met his violent end.

☼**27** By what shorter, headline-making name was this notorious Bronx mobster known?

8. On a January evening in 1909 Councilman E. P. Weeden of Trenton heard the flapping of wings and saw a cloven hoofprint in the snow on the roof of his porch.

☼**28** What is the name usually given to the strange bat-winged creature that many people have reported seeing over the years in southern New Jersey?

9. At the Battle of Gaines Mill in the Peninsular Campaign, the 4th New Jersey Regiment of the Army of the Potomac suffered heavy losses.

☼29 What Philadelphia-born future governor of New Jersey was in command of the entire Union Army of the Potomac during this Civil War campaign?

10. On February 6, 1951, a Pennsylvania Railroad commuter train, *The Broker*, southbound from New York City, derailed on a temporary wooden bridge, killing 84 people.

☼30 In what New Jersey township did this worst of modern U.S. railroad accidents occur?

BONUS PUZZLERS / 12

Monumental Events

a. A massive white monument stands at the corner of Nassau, Mercer, and Stockton Streets in Princeton. What event does it commemorate? (3 points)

b. In Jersey City's Bergen Square stands a statue marking the spot where the town of Bergen was established in 1660. Whom does the statue honor? (4 points)

c. A memorial in Wharton State Forest marks the site where Capt. Emilio Carranza of Mexico died. What were the circumstances of his death? (5 points)

d. A marble marker at the St. Peter's Episcopal Church Burial Ground in Perth Amboy honors Thomas Mundy Peterson and the event that brought him recognition. What was the event? (5 points)

e. "The Father of Labor Day" is buried near Pennsauken. Who is this man who also helped found the American Federation of Labor? (3 points)

[20-point total—answers on page 127]

Buildings

Some of the buildings dealt with in these ten questions are still standing. Others are not. All are a part of the fascinating story of New Jersey, and several of them involve the broader history of the nation.

1. Cape May, the nation's oldest seaside resort, has hundreds of preserved or restored Victorian homes. One classic 18-room mansion is now a museum.

   ☼31 What is the name of this Victorian mansion in Cape May that was designed by Frank Furness?

2. In the words of the Rodgers and Hart song, "There's a small hotel, with a wishing well." And indeed there is. The inn, in a town on the Delaware River, still exists.

   ☼32 The first word in the name of the small hotel is *Colligan's*. What are the last two words?

3. Boxwood Hall in Elizabeth is a house steeped in history. George Washington, Alexander Hamilton, and the Marquis de Lafayette stayed here.

   ☼33 One owner of this house was president of the Continental Congress in 1782-83. Who is he?

4. For two seasons in the mid-1850s the imposing Mount Vernon Hotel was the world's largest. It contained more than 3,000 rooms.

   ☼34 In what New Jersey resort city was this vast frame hotel, which was destroyed by fire in 1856?

5. The Frelinghuysens have long been important in New Jersey political life. Theodorus came to America in 1719. Rodney was elected to Congress in 1994.

☼35 By what name is Whippany Farm, a 127-acre estate with a Colonial Revival home, now known?

6. Stagecoach travel in New Jersey's early history relied on inns for overnight travelers. Scotch Plains has such an inn that still stands, though now as a restaurant.

☼36 What is the name of this inn at the corner of Front Street and Park Avenue that was once a stagecoach stop on the Swift-Sure Stagecoach line?

7. One of the attractions in Ringwood State Park is a 78-room mansion that for nearly two centuries was home to a number of well-known people.

☼37 What is the name of this mansion in which inventor Peter Cooper and industrialist Abram S. Hewitt once lived?

8. New Jersey has several houses dating from the 1600s, a number of them in Monmouth County. One such home is on Kings Highway in Middletown.

☼38 This Dutch cottage was built in 1686, "enlarged in the English taste" in the mid-1700s, restored in 1936 and again in the late 1990s. What is it called?

9. In 1923 Colonel and Mrs. Kuser of Bernardsville gave the state thousands of acres in the Kittatinny Mountains. Included in the gift was their summer home, a large frame building in a spectacular setting.

☼**39** What was the original name of the Kuser mansion, built in 1888?

10. When financier Jay Gould's son decided to sell his estate in Lakewood, the Sisters of Mercy, then in Plainfield, purchased it to create a college campus.

☼**40** What is the name of the Catholic college that now occupies the old Gould estate?

BONUS PUZZLERS / 13

A Quintet of Courthouses

a. Gutzon Borglum's seated statue of Abraham Lincoln stands outside this marble courthouse that filmmakers were not allowed to use for *Bonfire of the Vanities*. What county is it in? (3 points)

b. Courthouses are sometimes known for their notorious cases. This one is. It's where the Lindbergh trial took place. What is the county? (3 points)

c. This yellow brick courthouse, opened in 1796, is believed to be the oldest courthouse in the U.S. still used by county courts. The county? (5 points)

d. Forget tradition. This modern, glass-walled courthouse rose in 1960 and the old one, dating to 1841, was demolished. The county? (4 points)

e. At 22 stories, 310 feet high, it's the tallest courthouse in New Jersey. What county is it in? (4 points)

[20-point total—answers on page 128]

Businesses

New Jersey is a beehive of business activity. Some of the largest multinational corporations have headquarters or facilities here. The ten questions that follow concern both present and past businesses in the state.

1. The Great Atlantic & Pacific Tea Co., better known as A&P, is one of the top employers in New Jersey. The company also is headquartered here.

    ☼41 What Bergen County town is home to A&P, the granddaddy of supermarket chains?

2. The company that makes Snickers candy bars and M&Ms has a facility in a parklike campus on Route 517 north of Hackettstown.

    ☼42 What is the name of this company—which is also the name of one of its most popular candy bars?

3. Restaurants are businesses, too, and New Jersey has many superb ones. High on everyone's list is this classy place on Prospect Avenue in West Orange.

    ☼43 What is the name of this restaurant whose grounds feature formal gardens and waterfalls?

4. Nabisco, Inc., produces SnackWells, Oreos, Ritz crackers, Lifesavers, and a host of other foodstuffs. It has offices in East Hanover and Parsippany.

    ☼44 Nabisco also has a bakery in New Jersey, once popular with visiting school groups. Where is it?

5. This city is the home of the Colt revolver, the submarine, and the steam locomotive. It all began with Alexander Hamilton's Society of Usefull Manufactures.

☼45 What New Jersey city got its start because Alexander Hamilton was impressed by the power of a waterfall?

6. This Burlington County community was founded in 1904 as a company town to produce steel for the wire cable used in suspension bridges.

☼46 What is the name of this town, now part of Florence Township, that took its name from the man who designed the Brooklyn Bridge?

7. New Jersey has a small but flourishing wine industry. Some of the wineries are fairly new, but this is the oldest continuously operating one in the nation.

☼47 It was founded in the 1870s and weathered Prohibition by producing medicinal tonic that was 22% alcohol. What is the name of this winery?

8. Drivers on the Turnpike might conclude that oil refineries and chemical plants drive the state's economy. In fact, another, cleaner industry is dominant.

☼48 Among the smaller (but still sizable) companies in this booming business are Schering-Plough, Warner-Lambert, and Becton, Dickinson—all with New Jersey addresses. What is the industry?

9. On the piers and abutments of the oldest permanent bridge across the Delaware stands a bridge with a large, lighted sign. The sign carries a slogan.

   ☼49 What is the five-word slogan, chosen in 1910, that promotes the manufacturing strength of the city on the New Jersey side of the bridge?

10. Paramus is home to a company that sells toys—enough toys to put the company high on the list of total sales by companies based in New Jersey.

   ☼50 What is the name of this chain of stores? (a grammatically faulty name, to be sure, but the stores carry more toys than Santa Claus).

Photo Quiz 3. This impressive eagle stands in front of the East Hanover headquarters of one of the major American corporations having offices and plants in New Jersey. What is the corporation?

Places

There are two kinds of geography, physical and cultural. One deals principally with landforms, the other with people in their physical setting. These ten questions cover both kinds and stray a bit into other fields as well.

1. New Jersey's western border, the Delaware River, is bridged at many points. Some of the bridges, including this one in Sussex County, replaced ferries.

   ☼51 What is the name of this private toll bridge near Layton that carries the name of the prior ferry?

2. A community sometimes tries to improve its image by adopting a new name. Thus, Pridmore's Swamp became New Brunswick.

   ☼52 What was Elmwood Park called before its residents decided to change its name?

3. When you live in a particular county, you know its county seat. Otherwise, you may find a county seat harder to name than the capital of Kazakhstan.

   ☼53 What, for example, is the county seat of Gloucester County?

4. All geographical names signify something, although many are commonplace. Some names, on the other hand, are curious enough to beg for an explanation.

   ☼54 A small town on the Maurice River is called Bivalve. Why is it called that?

5. In the middle of the Pine Barrens is the tiny village of Whitesbog. Its name gives a clue to the main crops grown in the surrounding region.

☼55 One of the crops grown near Whitesbog is blueberries The other, a well-known New Jersey bog crop, is what?

6. If you have studied a New Jersey road map, you may not be surprised by the answer to this question. But a pure guess is almost sure to be wrong.

☼56 What city in New Jersey has the largest geographical area?

7. The Dutch were among the early settlers in northeastern New Jersey. A few Dutch place names remain, although far fewer than in New York State.

☼57 In what county—whose cities include Tenafly and Hasbrouck Heights—was the Dutch presence especially notable?

8. New Jersey's official nickname is the Garden State. In earlier days it was sometimes called the Camden and Amboy State, after the railroad of that name.

☼58 Earlier yet New Jerseyans occasionally referred to their state as the Jersey Blue State. What prompted that nickname?

9. There is a highly forgettable 1977 movie called *New York, New York*. By contrast, two fine movies have this New Jersey shore city in their title.

☼**59** What New Jersey city provides the title for a 1944 musical starring Constance Moore and a 1980 film starring Burt Lancaster and Susan Sarandon?

10. In the 1830s this village, then called Monmouth Furnace, was a bustling part of the bog-iron industry. When the industry died, so did the community.

☼**60** What is the name of this village, now a state park, that made the iron pipes for New York City's first waterworks?

BONUS PUZZLERS / 14

Here, There, and All Over

a. Name four towns in New Jersey that have the same names as large foreign cities. (1 point each)

b. Name four European countries that have fewer people than the state of New Jersey (1990 Census: 7,879,164). (1 point each)

c. Name four towns in New Jersey whose train stations have become restaurants. (1 point each)

d. Name four county seats in New Jersey that have fewer than 10,000 people. (1 point each)

e. Name four towns in New Jersey that include the word *port.* (1 point each)

[20-point total—answers on page 128]

ANSWERS TO PHOTO QUIZ

1. Holland Township 2. Seaside Heights 3. Nabisco, Inc.
4. Newton (Sussex County) 5. Sandy Hook Light

Religion and Education

Public education (but not private schools and colleges) must observe the Constitutional separation of church and state. In New Jersey's early history the two endeavors were considered one—merged, as they are in this set of questions.

1. One-room schoolhouses have had a higher survival rate in New Jersey than, say, covered bridges. You can find examples in Millville, Florham Park, Vincentown.

   ☼61 In what Burlington County town is the state's oldest schoolhouse, where John Brainerd once taught?

2. The religious and educational work of Elizabeth Ann Bayley Seton, a convert to Catholicism, is honored in the names of two institutions of higher learning.

   ☼62 What two New Jersey institutions of higher learning have names honoring Mother Seton?

3. Few prep schools have the names of public universities attached to them. One that does in the oldest preparatory school in New Jersey.

   ☼63 What is the school in Somerset from which Joyce Kilmer, who wrote "Trees," graduated?

4. American history has many references to Puritans and Calvinists. But the descendents of these Protestant groups go by other names.

   ☼64 In New England many heirs to this tradition are Congregationalists. What are they in New Jersey?

5. One president of Princeton University went on to become governor of New Jersey. A later governor reversed the process, becoming a college president.

☼65 What governor of New Jersey became president of Drew University after his two terms in Trenton?

6. A number of New Jersey high schools can boast student averages higher than 1,000 on the SAT. Few, however, show better than an 1,100 average.

☼66 In 1993 a high school in an upscale 19th-century Morris County real-estate-development community topped the 1,100 mark on SATs. What school did it?

7. A brick church in Burlington, Old St. Mary's, is one of the oldest in the state, dating from 1703. Despite the name, it is not a Roman Catholic church.

☼67 What Protestant denomination worships in this church, using a silver communion service that was a gift from England's Queen Anne?

8. Very few high schools report 100% of their students getting passing grades on all three parts of the High School Proficiency Test (HSPT).

☼68 Of the four schools that turned in 100% HSPT performances in 1993, one is an urban high school in Hudson County. What is the name of the school?

9. John Woolman, a Mount Holly tailor and shopkeeper who became a minister, preached throughout the colonies. His great cause was antislavery.

☼69 To what "inner-light" Protestant denomination did this pioneering 18th-century antislavery crusader belong?

10. Thirteen monogrammed stones from the Church on the Green in Hackensack date back to 1696, although the present structure was built in 1791.

☼70 This church is an example of the Stone Dutch architectural style. What Protestant denomination worships in it?

BONUS PUZZLERS / 15

Oh, Alma Mater

a. What New Jersey college or university has teams that go by the name of Knights? (4 points)

b. Princeton University's colors are orange and black. What other college or university in the Garden State has teams that wear orange and black? (4 points)

c. Which New Jersey college or university has teams that answer to the name of The Pirates? (3 points)

d. Rutgers University sends the Scarlet Knights to do battle with rival powers. What New Jersey team sends the Gothic Knights? (5 points)

e. When Trenton State athletes sally forth to the fray, what lordly beasts do they deign to call themselves? (4 points)

[20-point total—answers on page 128]

Sports

New Jersey has had professional baseball in Newark and Jersey City and even in little Bloomingdale. It has produced world boxing champions in nearly every weight class and has been home to stars in virtually all sports.

1. This basketball player, a native of Union City, starred for Holy Cross College from 1954 to 1956. Next year he joined the Boston Celtics.

☼71 Who is this basketball great who spent his entire career with the then all-but-unbeatable Celtics?

2. Born in Camden, South Carolina, raised in Paterson, this baseball outfielder was the first African American to play in the American League.

☼72 He broke in with the Cleveland Indians on July 5, 1947. Who is he?

3. AFC Rookie of the Year in 1972 and a star running back for the Pittsburgh Steelers, he was raised in Mount Holly and played college football at Penn State.

☼73 Who is this Pro Football Hall of Famer, one of the NFL's all-time career leaders in rushing?

4. New Jersey fielded two standout teams in the old Negro Leagues. One of them was the Newark Eagles. The other was very good, too.

☼74 What Negro League team in New Jersey numbered among its stars Dick Lundy and Pop Lloyd?

5. This welterweight boxer, born in Elizabeth, fighting out of Union, held the world championship in his weight class from 1941 to 1946.

☼75 He won the welterweight title in a 15-round decision over Fritzie Zivic at Ruppert Stadium in Newark. Who is he?

6. Born in West Orange in 1863 and a graduate of Orange High School, this football coach was named Coach of the Year in 1943 at the age of 81.

☼76 Who is this remarkable coach who established his reputation at the University of Chicago before moving on, at age 70, to the College of the Pacific?

7. New Jersey had a major league baseball team for one season, 1915: the Newark Peppers (or Peps) in a short-lived league that challenged the NL and AL.

☼77 What is the name of this league that survived for only two seasons just prior to World War I?

8. This Princeton quarterback, five-feet-eleven, 170 pounds, was a unanimous choice for All-American in both his junior and senior years.

☼78 Who is this quarterback who in 1951 won the Heisman Trophy by the biggest margin up to then in the history of the award?

9. A lifelong New Jersey resident—he was born in Salem and died in Bridgeton—he played the outfield for the Washington Senators, batting .379 in 1928.

☼**79** Who is this Hall of Fame ballplayer, who, after his playing days were over, managed the Trenton team of the Inter-State League for several seasons?

10. A boxing legend, he held the welterweight title from 1922 to 1926 and the middleweight title from 1926 to 1931—a ten-year championship reign.

☼**80** They called this Elizabeth-born boxer the "Toy Bulldog." Who is he?

Baseball outfielder Joe (Ducky) Medwick, born in Carteret, wasted no time on his way to the major leagues. He starred for the St. Louis Cardinals in the Gas House Gang era of the 1930s. A .324 career hitter, Medwick was named to baseball's Hall of Fame in 1968.

Superlatives

New Jersey is the most densely populated state in the nation, and it offers several other things that rank as the first, the biggest, the tallest, the best—or even the opposite: the last, the worst, etc. These question cover ten of them.

1. New Jersey was the third state to ratify the U.S. Constitution. It was the first state to ratify another key document in American history.

   ☼81   What basic document of American freedom was New Jersey the first to adopt?

2. Newspaper circulation may reflect the size of a city, but not always. In New Jersey, three of the top papers are from Hackensack, Asbury Park, and Camden.

   ☼82   The New Jersey newspaper with the largest circulation *does* come from the largest city. What is it?

3. The worst disaster in New Jersey (after the 1854 shipwreck at Ship Bottom) took 326 lives when three German ocean liners caught fire while docked.

   ☼83   The fire broke out on June 30, 1900. In what New Jersey city did it happen?

4. When you put a roll of film in your camera, you benefit from the ingenuity of a Newark inventor who found a substitute for light-sensitized glass plates.

   ☼84   Who is this Newark man who back in 1887 applied for a patent for flexible photographic film?

5. There was a time when this Sussex County town was the leading producer of zinc in the United States. Today it is better known for its fluorescent minerals.

☼85 What is the name of this town that now features a mineral museum, including a replica of a mine?

6. The historic district of this city is New Jersey's largest, consisting of some 2,200 Colonial, Federal, and Victorian buildings.

☼86 What is this city on the Cohansey River that has its own liberty bell, struck in 1763 and rung to announce the Declaration of Independence?

7. The first English settlement in New Jersey is now the largest city in Union County. Dating from 1664, it began with a name very close to its present one.

☼87 What was the first settlement in the state, named the same today as it was then, except that -town has been dropped?

8. State records for game fish change over the years, as do the places where the fish are caught. Several record fish have been taken from the Delaware River.

☼88 As of 1995, the record smallmouth bass, American eel, brown trout, and lake trout were all caught in the same body of water. What is it?

9. On June 15, 1776, the last royal governor of New Jersey was arrested at his home in Perth Amboy after refusing the option of tacitly supporting the American Revolution.

☼**89** Who is this colonial governor, the illegitimate son of a great American stateman, who remained loyal to the Crown during the Revolutionary War?

10. In a ZIP code directory of New Jersey, *Absecon* is the first alphabetical listing.

☼**90** What is the last ZIP code listing under New Jersey? (It is the only *Z* included.)

BONUS PUZZLERS / 16

The Last Name's the Same

a. Kenneth ---- was the first black mayor of Newark. Althea ----, from East Orange, was the first black tennis player to win at Wimbledon. Both have the same last name. What is it? (3 points)

b. Mary Mapes ---- wrote *Hans Brinker and the Silver Skates*. Geraldine R. ---- owned Giralda Farms in Madison. What is the shared last name? (3 points)

c. John ---- came from a family of great Hoboken inventors. Willie ---- was one of the defendants in the Hall-Mills murder case. Their last name? (5 points)

d. Sandra ----, an actress from Bayonne, made her best-known films as a teenager. Leo ---- is a Maplewood artist. Their last name? (5 points)

e. John ----, a famous writer, is buried in Princeton Cemetery. Mary ---- is the author of *My Friend Flicka*. Their last name? (4 points)

[20-point total—answers on page 128)

The Arts

Did you know that Nathanael West completed his novel *Miss Lonelyhearts* at what is now the Frenchtown Inn (then called the Warford House) in Frenchtown? No? Not to worry. The questions that follow are a bit easier—though none too easy.

1. Frank and Lillian Gilbreth, efficiency experts (as they needed to be), raised their 12 children on Eagle Rock Way in Montclair.

   ☼**91** What well-known book did two of the Gilbreth children write about their experiences growing up?

2. The cartoonist Charles Addams, famous for his classic *New Yorker* cartoons that inspired the *Addams Family* films, was a native New Jerseyan.

   ☼**92** In what New Jersey community did Charles Addams live and work?

3. One of the outstanding painters, graphic artists, and book illustrators of the 1930s lived in Roosevelt. His art deals with social and political themes.

   ☼**93** Who is this New Jersey artist, whose finest work includes *The Passion of Sacco and Vanzetti?*

4. For years this black theater group occupied the upstairs of a rather run-down building in New Brunswick. Now it is next to the George Street Playhouse.

   ☼**94** What is the name of this celebrated black theater company?

5. In 1888 this English author spent six weeks in Manasquan, working on his latest novel at the old Union House.

☼**95** Who is the world-famous author who wrote part of *The Master of Ballantrae* while at the Jersey Shore?

6. The movie *Ragtime*, starring James Cagney in his last role, was filmed partly at the magnificent Essex-Sussex beach hotel.

☼**96** What is the New Jersey resort community in which E. L. Doctorow's novel is brought to life on the screen?

7. Two of the best art museums in New Jersey are at universities—the Princeton Art Museum and the Jane Voorhees Zimmerli Art Museum at Rutgers.

☼**97** Another fine art museum is in an Essex County community of 38,000 people. It is not connected with a university. What is its name?

8. Born in Hoboken in 1864, this great photographer, more than any other person, brought about the recognition of photography as a fine art.

☼**98** Who is this man who in 1905 established his famous gallery "291" at 291 Fifth Avenue, New York City, exhibiting photographs as art?

9. Like many other fine stage productions, *Having Our Say*, starring Gloria Foster and Mary Alice, had its

world premier at this New Jersey theater before opening on Broadway.

☼99 What is this theater on University Avenue in Princeton that won a Tony Award for Outstanding Regional Theater in 1994?

10. One of the Metropolitan Opera's greatest sopranos was born in Montclair in 1915. A versatile performer, she made her mark not only in grand opera but also in concert tours and on radio and televison.

☼100 Who is this glamorous prima donna who appeared with Mario Lanza in the 1951 film *The Great Caruso?*

Answers to Bonus Puzzlers 5 to 8

5 / WEALTH FROM THE EARTH   **a.** zinc   **b.** iron   **c.** Lumberton   **d.** uranium   **e.** quartz

6 / CLINTON—NAMED FOR BILL?   **a.** Neptune   **b.** Sparta   **c.** Wayne   **d.** Garfield   **e.** Cape May Court House   **f.** Alpha   **g.** Whitehouse or White House Station   **h.** Deal   **i.** Colts Neck   **j.** Gladstone

7 / TEAMS PAST AND PRESENT   **a.** New Jersey Generals   **b.** Newark Eagles   **c.** New Jersey Devils   **d.** Seton Hall   **e.** Jersey City Giants

8 / WE'RE NUMBER ONE!   **a.** Roselle   **b.** Paterson   **c.** Pine Barrens   **d.** Hoboken   **e.** High Point State Park

Photo Quiz 4. Many county seats have monuments honoring the soldiers who fought in the U.S. Civil War. It is sometimes hard to tell them apart. In what county seat does the Civil War monument in this photo stand?

Oh, the questions that might have been asked! All those name changes, for example. Ah, well. On to the answers.

Answers

☞ The Basic Quiz

pages 77 to 102

☼ The Super Quiz

pages 103 to 127

Photo Quiz 5. There are many lighthouses along the New Jersey coastline. This one is the oldest operating lighthouse in the United States, having guided ships at sea since 1764. Which lighthouse is it?

Answers ☞1 to ☞10 / Entertainers

☞ 1   Lou Costello

Lou Costello, born Louis Cristillo in Paterson, and Bud Abbott, born William Abbott in Asbury Park, were a successful vaudeville comedy team before making their transition to the movies. The pair achieved great popularity with their films for Universal Pictures in the 1940s. The lean, nervous Abbott (1895-1974) played the brash, none too bright straight man, while the fat, hapless Lou Costello (1906-1959) was a bit denser than his partner and the butt of the jokes.

☞ 2   Paul Robeson

The son of a runaway slave who became a minister in Princeton, Paul Robeson (1898-1976) attended Rutgers College, graduated first in his class, won All-American honors in football, and went on to Columbia Law School. He made his acting debut in 1924 with the Provincetown Players and appeared as a concert singer the next year. Although he was widely admired as a singer and actor, his association with Communist causes angered many.

☞ 3   Frank Sinatra

Born in Hoboken in 1915, Frank Sinatra gained fame as a singer with the Harry James and Tommy Dorsey bands in the late 1930s and early '40s. A scrawny kid with a casual, romantic style, he wowed the bobby-soxers, who screamed and swooned while he performed. A hugely popular singer, he also became an accomplished actor, winning plaudits for his role in the 1956 film *The Man with the Golden Arm* and many others. Some called him "The Chairman of the Board."

☞ 4   Eva Marie Saint

This delicate-looking actress, born in Newark in 1924, began her career in radio and television dramas. She attracted attention by winning the Drama Critics Award for her role in the 1953 Broadway show *The Trip to Bountiful.* But early success on stage and screen did not translate into continuing star status. She returned to the New York stage in 1983 after a decade's absence.

☞ 5 Connie Francis

Born Concetta Franconero in Newark in 1938, Connie Francis won first prize on Arthur Godfrey's *Talent Scouts* at the age of 12 and went on to become one of the most popular female singers of all time. She lost her voice after a brutal rape in a Long Island motel in 1974. It took her years to recover for a comeback. Her autobiography, *Who's Sorry Now,* was published in 1984.

☞ 6 Jack Nicholson

After playing in several Roger Corman cheapies, Jack Nicholson got his big break in the 1969 film *Easy Rider.* A succession of triumphs followed, including Oscars as Best Actor in *One Flew over the Cuckoo's Nest* and Best Supporting Actor in *Terms of Endearment.* A versatile performer who can play varying roles, he seems at his best as an outsider, a drifter bucking the system.

☞ 7 Bruce Springsteen

A rock singer, songwriter, guitarist, and bandleader, Bruce Springsteen, the only son of a working-class family, was born in Freehold in 1949. He worked in a number of local bands before recording his attention-grabbing first album in 1973. After the release in 1975 of *Born to Run,* he appeared on the covers of *Time* and *Newsweek.* Springsteen's first chart-topping album was *The River* in 1980, which also included his first top-ten single, "Hungry Heart." His *Born in the USA* album was a huge seller.

☞ 8 Meryl Streep

Meryl Streep was born Mary Louise Streep in Summit in 1949. She attended Vassar and the Yale School of Drama, making her screen debut in the 1977 film *Julia.* The next year she won an Academy Award nomination for her role in *The Deer Hunter.* Since then she has won two Oscars, as Best Actress in *Sophie's Choice* and as Best Supporting Actress in *Kramer vs. Kramer.*

☞ 9 Jon Bon Jovi

Born in 1962, his actual name is John Bongiovi. His New Jersey-based group, Bon Jovi, hit the top-40 charts with singles from the debut album, Bon Jovi, including "Runaway" and "She Don't Know Me." The group's third album on the Mercury label,

Slippery When Wet, came out in 1986 and moved up to number one on *Billboard* charts in early 1987. A cameo role in the 1990 film *Young Guns II* inspired his first solo album, *Blaze of Glory.*

☞ 10 Whitney Houston

Her mother, Cissy Houston, is also a singer. So is her aunt, Thelma Houston, and her cousin, Dionne Warwick. Born in Newark in 1963, Whitney Houston began singing as a child in the New Hope Baptist Junior Choir. As a model she appeared on the cover of *Seventeen.* She gained immediate fame—and huge sales—with her first album, *Whitney Houston,* in 1984, following it up with a succession of hit albums and singles.

Answers ☞11 to ☞20 / Movers and Shakers

☞ 11 Thomas A. Edison

One of the most productive inventors of all time, Thomas Alva Edison (1847-1931) was a genius at turning scientific principles to practical use. He was called the "Wizard of Menlo Park" for the New Jersey location of his first laboratory. Built in 1876, the lab is now at the Greenfield Village Museum in Dearborn, Michigan. Edison developed the incandescent lamp at Menlo Park. His second laboratory, in West Orange, established in 1887, is now the Edison National Historic Site. It was here, over a 44-year period, that he perfected the phonograph, motion picture camera, and electric storage battery.

☞ 12 Clara Barton

Born in Massachusetts, Clara Barton (1821-1912) opened one of New Jersey's first free public schools in 1852. Her schoolhouse still stands at 142 Crosswicks Street, Bordentown. When the Civil War broke out, she nursed in army camps and on the battlefield. Later, while in Europe during the Franco-Prussian war, she worked with the International Red Cross. Returning to the United States, she organized the American Red Cross in 1881 and headed it until 1904.

☛ 13   Grover Cleveland

Grover Cleveland, the 22nd and 24th President of the United States (Benjamin Harrison intervened), was born at 207 Bloomfield Avenue, Caldwell, now a State Historic Site. Cleveland (1837-1908) moved to Buffalo, New York, as a young man and served as mayor of that city and governor of New York before his election to the Presidency. In retirement, he returned to New Jersey, settling in Princeton, where he died. He is buried in Princeton Cemetery.

☛ 14:   William F. Halsey, Jr.

A five-star admiral, William F. "Bull" Halsey, Jr. (1882-1959) was born at 134 West Jersey Street, Elizabeth. A 1904 graduate of Annapolis, he gained notice in 1942 with a spectacular carrier raid against the Japanese in the Marshall Islands and Gilbert Islands. In 1944-45 he commanded the U.S. 3rd Fleet and led the sea-borne bombardment of Japan. One of the rest areas on the New Jersey Turnpike is named in his honor.

☛ 15:   Christine Todd Whitman

Christine Todd Whitman, born in New York City in 1946, came from behind in the preelection polls to turn back James Florio's bid for reelection as governor in 1993. A resident of Oldwick, Governor Whitman had been a freeholder in Somerset County and president of the State Board of Public Utilities. She gained prominence by nearly defeating an overconfident Senator Bill Bradley when he ran for reelection in 1990.

☛ 16   Woodrow Wilson

The 28th President of the United States, (Thomas) Woodrow Wilson (1856-1924), graduated from Princeton in 1879, returning to the university in 1890 as a professor of jurisprudence and political economy. He became the first nonclerical president of Princeton in 1902. In 1910 he ran for governor of New Jersey and won. Two years later he was nominated by the Democrats to run from President, and once again he won. A reformer and an idealist, leader of the nation in World War I, he ranks as one of our most influential Presidents.

☞ 17 Molly Pitcher

Born near Trenton, Mary Ludwig Hays (or perhaps Heis) (1744-1832), was the wife of a soldier at the Battle of Monmouth, June 28, 1778, in the American Revolution. As a result of her carrying water to her husband and the other parched Continental troops on the blazing hot battlefield that day, she earned the nickname Molly Pitcher. A plaque on the battlefield monument in Freehold honors her.

☞ 18 Albert Einstein

Albert Einstein (1879-1955) is recognized as one of the greatest physicists of all time. Born in Ulm, Germany, he had acquired international fame by the time he emigrated to the United States in the early 1930s to escape Nazism. Winner of the 1921 Nobel Prize in Physics, he continued his groundbreaking work at Princeton's Institute for Advanced Study until his death. His theory of relativity revolutionized physics. His research also led to the development of the atomic bomb.

☞ 19 Buzz Aldrin

Born Edwin E. Aldrin, Jr., in Montclair in 1930, Buzz Aldrin graduated from Montclair High School and the U.S. Military Academy in 1951. After flying 62 combat missions in Korea, he pursued graduate study in astronautics and in 1963 received his doctorate from MIT. He entered the space program later that year. In 1966 he piloted Gemini 12 and walked in space for more than five hours. In 1969, as an astronaut, he became the second person to set foot on the moon.

☞ 20 Milton Friedman

Milton Friedman, born in 1912, became a noted economics professor and writer, opposing government economic controls and rejecting Keynesian theories. At the University of Chicago and later at Stanford University's Hoover Institution on War, Revolution, and Peace, he promoted the revival of monetarist theories. In his book *Capitalism and Freedom,* published in 1962, he proposed a negative income tax, which would guarantee a minimum family income. Friedman advised President Ronald Reagan on economics.

Answers ☞21 to ☞30 / Events

☞ 21 Aaron Burr
Probably the most famous duel in American history occurred on that grassy shelf above the Hudson River in Weehawken, a notorious dueling site of the time. Aaron Burr (1756-1836), a long-time political foe of Alexander Hamilton, challenged the ex-Secretary of the Treasury to a duel. They met on July 11, 1804. Burr, born in Newark, a son of the second president of Princeton (then the College of New Jersey), shot and mortally wounded his foe. Hamilton died the next day. Burr fled south to avoid indictment.

☞ 22 *Morro Castle*
The *Morro Castle*, a Ward Line cruise ship returning from Havana, caught fire in the early morning hours off Sea Girt. The ship's captain, Robert R. Wilmott, had died unexpectedly about seven hours earlier, leaving the chief officer in command. Wind fanned the flames as the *Morro Castle* plowed northward. Finally, the burnt-out ship came to rest off Asbury Park, but by then 134 people had died.

☞ 23 Silk industry
In the mid-1800s Paterson became known as the "Silk City." Silk mills abounded. The industry reached its peak in 1910, when 350 plants employed 25,000 workers and manufactured nearly one third of the nation's silk. That stopped abruptly with the great silk strike of 1913. The owners responded with a lockout. Workers met at the Botto house in Haledon, now the American Labor Museum. Despite strong leadership, the silk strike failed, and workers went back to the new "two-loom" system they had so fervently opposed.

☞ 24 Lyndon B. Johnson and Alexei Kosygin
The Glassboro Summit in June 1967 was much publicized at the time. President Lyndon B. Johnson of the United States and Premier Alexei Kosygin of the Soviet Union met at Glassboro State College to try to ease Cold War tensions. People spoke hopefully at the time about the "Spirit of Glassboro."

☞ 25 Charles A. Lindbergh, Jr.

Charles A. Lindbergh, the daredevil aviator and world-famous "Lone Eagle," had moved to a secluded estate in Hopewell to find privacy from the press and public. His wife, the former Anne Morrow of Englewood, and their 20-month-old son, Charles, Jr., were with him on the night of March 1, 1932, when the infant was kidnapped from an upstairs bedroom. The baby was later found dead. A media circus followed, subsiding only after the execution in 1936 of Bruno Richard Hauptmann for the crime.

☞ 26 *Hindenburg*

The German airship *Hindenburg* was 250 feet off the ground, maneuvering toward its mooring mast at Lakehurst, when it burst into flames. Passengers and crew members leaped from the gondola or were burned alive as the giant dirigible was consumed by flames in about four minutes. Thirty-six people, including one ground crew worker, died in this disaster.

☞ 27 Morris Canal

New Jersey's canal-building era was brief but feverish. Mining in Pennsylvania and northwestern New Jersey provided much of the impetus for constructing the Morris Canal, which was completed in 1831 at a cost of $2,850,000. It proved unprofitable. An insufficient channel along with the growth of railroads doomed the canal within a decade. The canal bed still exists in some places and is often marked. Waterloo Village near Stanhope was a port on the Morris Canal, and a towpath and lock remain. A small museum at Waterloo details the history of the canal.

☞ 28 Battle of Trenton

Although the Leutze painting is often criticized for its historical inaccuracy, the actual event was every bit as heroic as George Washington's pose in the boat. The Continental army, recently in retreat to Pennsylvania, struck back across the ice-choked Delaware, crossing some 2,500 troops on Christmas night, 1776, and attacking the Hessian troops quartered in Trenton the next day. The surprise and the victory were complete. Eight days later Washington followed up this success with a win over the British at Princeton.

☞ 29   Teterboro Airport

This airport, the second busiest in New Jersey, takes up most of the tiny municipality, whose permanent population hovers around 20. The Aviation Hall of Fame & Museum at the airport consists of two parts—one, the old control tower with memorabilia from the early days of New Jersey flying; the other, an educational center with larger aviation displays.

☞ 30   Grovers Mill

Orson Welles' connection with New Jersey is the celebrated radio broadcast he made from New York City on October 30, 1938. His vivid dramatization of H. G. Wells science-fiction classic *The War of the Worlds* threw many listeners into a frenzy. The Martians were landing, Welles' "correspondents" assured the audience, near tiny Grovers Mill, New Jersey.

Answers ☞31 to ☞40 / Buildings

☞ 31   Ford Mansion

General George Washington with his wife Martha spent the winter of 1779-80 in this Georgian mansion in Morristown while his troops were encamped at nearby Jockey Hollow. The mansion had been completed in 1774 by Colonel Jacob Ford, Jr., a well-to-do businessman who produced gunpowder for the Continental army. Colonel Ford served briefly in the army himself, dying in 1777 of smallpox. His widow rented the house to the army for the use of the Washingtons.

☞ 32   Walt Whitman House

The Walt Whitman House State Historic Site, a modest home at 330 Mickle Street in Camden, is the only house the poet ever owned. Whitman spent the last years of his life here, from 1884 to 1892, devoting much of his time to revising his masterpiece, *Leaves of Grass*, and publishing new editions. Before moving to the house, he had lived in Camden for many years.

☞ 33 Old Barracks

During the French and Indian War, the New Jersey Colonial Assembly authorized the building of five barracks to house Colonial troops that had previously been quartered in private homes. This is the only one still standing. In the Revolution the barracks changed hands with the fortunes of war, most notably after the Battle of Trenton. After the war it served a variety of purposes before being restored for use as a museum.

☞ 34 Long Branch

The reason St. James Chapel was attended by so many U.S. Presidents is that Long Branch was a summer resort to rival Saratoga Springs in the late 19th century—indeed, through World War I—and Washington, D.C., was not far away. The seven Presidents who attended the church were Ulysses S. Grant, Rutherford B. Hayes, James A. Garfield, Chester A. Arthur, Benjamin Harrison, William McKinley, and Woodrow Wilson. In 1881 President Garfield died at the nearby Elberon Hotel, after being shot in the nation's capital.

☞ 35 Morven

At 55 Stockton Street in Princeton, this impressive Georgian house was the home of Richard Stockton, a signer of the Declaration of Independence. Former Governor Walter E. Edge donated the house in 1951 for use as a governor's mansion, and it was so used from 1954 to 1982. Morven is now a museum run by the New Jersey State Museum.

☞ 36 Resorts International

The first of Atlantic City's legal gambling palaces opened on May 27, 1978, at the corner of North Carolina Avenue and Boardwalk. It debuted less than three months after Governor Brendan Byrne signed legislation permitting a temporary license. Resorts, a key player in the pro-casino campaign that ended in a successful referendum in the election of 1976, moved quickly to open its casino hotel, keeping the facade of the old Chalfonte-Haddon Hall. Since 1989 it has been Merv Griffin's Resorts Casino Hotel.

☛ 37 Barnegat Ligthhouse

Old Barney, as it is often called, was first lit in 1859. An earlier lighthouse on the same site, dating from the 1834, fell into the sea. George Gordon Meade, a military engineer before the Civil War brought him fame, designed the present structure, a 167-foot red-and-white tower with 217 steps leading to a lookout that offers spectacular views of the beach and ocean. The lighthouse is one of the most photographed attractions in New Jersey.

☛ 38 Monmouth College

Approximately 3,800 students attend Monmouth College, a private four-year institution founded in 1933. The college benefited from the Depression-era breakup of New Jersey's elegant estates. Much of its 125-acre campus was once the Guggenheim estate. Shadow Lawn, a limestone mansion modeled on Versailles, stands on the site of President Woodrow Wilson's summer home, which burned. The 130-room mansion, with its three-story great hall, was built in 1929.

☛ 39 Clairmont Diner, Tick Tock Diner

Both diners are on Route 3 West in Clifton. The Clairmont is sleekly modern; the Tick Tock is somewhat old-fashioned. Both are large and busy, with menus that seem to be compilations of every other diner menu in existence. Both have won consistent praise from road-food buffs. New Jersey, partly because of its history as a manufacturer of diners, has long been regarded as "the diner capital of the world."

☛ 40 Burlington

The Burlington County Historical Society is housed in James Fenimore Cooper's birthplace at 457 High Street. Cooper, whose family moved to upstate New York not long after his birth in 1789, is the author of *The Last of the Mohicans* and four other *Leather-Stocking Tales*. Next door, in a house that shares a common wall, is the birthplace of James Lawrence, naval officer in command of the *Chesapeake* in the War of 1812. Born in 1781 at 459 High Street, Lawrence is famous for his dying order in 1813: "Don't give up the ship."

Answers ☞41 to ☞50 / Businesses

☞ 41 Johnson & Johnson

Johnson & Johnson has more than kept pace with the explosive growth in the health-care industry. Beginning as a tiny business in 1886 with 14 employees, it expanded over its first hundred years to become a multinational corporation of 160 companies in 55 countries. Architect I. M. Pei designed J&J's present worldwide corporate headquarters in downtown New Brunswick. The corporation's consumer products are a litany of familiar names, not only Band-Aids and Tylenol but also Johnson's Baby Powder, Baby Shampoo, Dental Floss, Red Cross Cotton Balls, and so on.

☞ 42 Mercer

At one time the automobile industry had real vitality in New Jersey, producing the Star in Elizabeth, the Simplex in New Brunswick, the Phianna in Newark, and the Mercer in Trenton, county seat of Mercer County. The Mercer, manufactured from 1910 to 1925, achieved a considerable reputation. The 1911 Type 35 Raceabout, with its 70-mile per-hour guaranteed top speed, was a very sporty machine.

☞ 43 Colgate-Palmolive Co.

One of the earliest companies to shift its manufacturing operations from New York City to New Jersey was the Colgate Company, founded by William Colgate in 1806. Colgate moved his soap-making factory to Jersey City in 1847. The gigantic Colgate clock, erected to replace an earlier, smaller one, dates from 1924. In 1928 the company merged with the Palmolive-Peet Company, creating one of the largest soap manufacturers in the world. Today it is a diversified company, perhaps best known for dentifrices and deodorants.

☞ 44 Campbell Soup Company

The Campbell Soup Company began not with canned soup but with fancy peas and tomatoes. Joseph Campbell and Abram A. Anderson founded their company in 1869, but soaring success awaited the arrival of chemist John T. Dorrance in 1897. The innovative Dorrance dreamed up the idea and developed the process for condensing soup. In time it made him president of the company and a multimillionaire. Today the company, dominant in the soup market, also makes other products.

☞ 45 Ballantine

In the 19th and early 20th centuries Newark was known for its breweries. One of the largest of these, the Ballantine Brewery, was founded in 1840 by Peter Ballantine, a Scot. In 1885 his son, John Ballantine, built the eclectic but exquisite Ballantine House. Older New York Yankee fans will recall sportscaster Mel Allen waxing enthusiastic over a "Ballantine blast," which is to say, a home run.

☞ 46 Bell Labs

Bell Telephone Laboratories is recognized as one of the foremost electronics research centers in the world. Established at Murray Hill in 1942, Bell Labs has helped shape our electronics universe. Among the research center's many Nobel Prize winners are the inventors of the transistor: John Bardeen, Walter H. Brattain, and William Shockley.

☞ 47 Motion picture industry

The Great Train Robbery, a pioneering silent movie was filmed in 1903 in Caldwell. It was eleven minutes long, a full-length feature of the day. The Palisades, near to Fort Lee, proved a popular site for filming. *Rescued from an Eagle's Nest* came out in 1908, with the soon-to-be-famous director D. W. Griffith playing a lowly mountaineer. Many early movie stars appeared in films made in or near Fort Lee, including Rudolph Valentino, Charlie Chaplin, and Lillian Gish. New Jersey seemed to have the film industry well in hand, but by the early 1920s it had moved to California.

☞ 48 Allied-Signal Inc.

In the 1980s this aerospace company outpaced all other companies in New Jersey in total sales. But in the early 1990s, with the end of the Cold War and the aging of the American population, it began losing its top spot (by a whisker) to health-care giant Johnson & Johnson. Still, with nearly $12 billion in annual sales and with 4,500 employees in New Jersey (almost 100,000 worldwide), Allied-Signal is no mom-and-pop enterprise.

☞ 49 Prudential Insurance Company of America

This is by no means New Jersey's only insurance company. Mutual Benefit Life, for example, goes back to 1845, while John F. Dryden's Pru got its start 30 years later, in 1875, in Newark. The Pru has grown considerably since then. Indeed, it is the nation's largest insurance company and has branched out into several other fields.

☞ 50 Merck & Company, Inc.

This diverse company is in the business of discovering, developing, producing, and marketing human and animal health products and specialty chemicals. George Merck, the company's founder, completed construction of a three-story brick building in Rahway in 1903. The company has been growing ever since. A Merck & Company research center was built in 1933, setting the trend for such facilities in New Jersey.

Answers ☞51 to ☞60 / Places

☞ 51 Perth Amboy

A colonial seaport dating back to 1651, Perth Amboy was settled by the Dutch. First known as Ambo Point, its growth began in 1685 when the Earl of Perth allowed 200 downtrodden Scots to emigrate to the spot. They named it New Perth, but eventually the mixed name Perth Amboy caught on. In 1686 the town became the provincial capital of East New Jersey. In 1718 Perth Amboy received the charter that makes it the oldest incorporated city in the state. Most of the colony's royal governors lived in Perth Amboy.

☞ 52 Hackensack

Hackensack was first settled by Dutch traders from Manhattan in the 1640s. But since two early settlers holding large tracts of land came from Barbadoes, the city was officially called New Barbadoes until 1921. The name *Hackensack* is Indian, although no one is quite sure of the original pronunciation or meaning. During the Revolutionary War, both British and Continental troops camped on Hackensack's Green. Today one of the largest-circulation newspapers, *The Record*, is published here.

☞ 53 Red Bank

Early in its history Red Bank, whose name apparently comes from the color of the clay along the Navesink River, served as a bustling port, trading goods regularly with New York City. Passenger steamship service between Red Bank and New York existed for nearly 100 years, from the 1830s to the 1920s. Edmund Wilson, the famous literary critic, was born in Red Bank in 1895. Count Basie, the renowned jazz musician, also a Red Bank native, was born in 1904. The huge uniform-manufacturing company founded in 1885 by Sigmund Eisner occupied five buildings in town, which have now been converted to a commerical complex.

☞ 54 Salem

No county in the state is more rural than Salem, despite the Delaware Memorial Bridge and the Salem nuclear reactor. First settled by Swedes, Finns, and a few Dutch, the county became predominantly Quaker early in its history. The county seat, Salem, was the first permanent English settlement in West New Jersey. The huge Salem Oak that stands in the middle of the Friends' burial ground may have been living when Columbus set sail.

☞ 55 Kearny

When the Civil War began, the North could hardly have asked for a better field commander than Hudson County's Philip Kearny. A veteran of the Mexican War, where he had lost his left arm, he had also fought with the French in Italy, winning the Legion of Honor at Solferino. In the Civil War he initially led New Jersey's first volunteer brigade, consisting of the 1st, 2nd, 3rd, and 4th infantry regiments. A new community carved from Harrison in 1867 took his name.

☞ 56 Ocean Grove

Founded in 1869 for Methodist camp meetings, Ocean Grove became famous for its blue laws. The streets were closed to Sunday traffic in the most effective way possible—gates leading into town were closed. Pilgrims to Ocean Grove used to pitch their tents in town, prompting the sobriquet "Tent City." Ocean Grove is just one of the shore towns founded by Methodists. Two others are Asbury Park and Bradley Beach.

☞ 57 Burlington

This question could have been worded differently: What is New Jersey's largest county? The answer is the same. Burlington. The area of the county was once much greater than it is today, but even after being reduced, it remains number one in size by a wide margin. Much of the famed Pine Barrens, although not all of it, lies within Burlington County.

☞ 58 Madison

One of Morris County's most attractive towns, Madison has two colleges, a popular museum (Museum of Early Trades and Crafts), and an elegant municipal building (a gift from Mrs. Geraldine R. Dodge). The town was once the nation's rose capital. At the height of the industry, Madison greenhouses were producing 25 million roses a year. The earlier name of the community, Bottle Hill, echoed the name of a local tavern.

☞ 59 Roosevelt

Planners at the Federal Resettlement Administration laid out the town in the 1930s as a utopian community, with a cooperative factory, a cooperative store, and communal farms. Like most other utopian ventures, it worked better in theory than in practice. Today the Monmouth County town still has some of the original structures.

☞ 60 Jersey City

Liberty State Park stands on acreage that as late as the 1970s was abandoned railroad yards. Morris Pesin, a Jersey City native, led the drive to have the state acquire the land and create the park. The imposing Central Railroad of New Jersey Terminal, built in

1899 and renovated as part of the renewal project, is on the grounds, as is the highly praised Liberty Science Center.

Answers ☞61 to ☞70 / Religion and Education

☞ 61 Rutgers University
Strictly speaking, the institution is "Rutgers: The State University of New Jersey," with various campuses in New Brunswick and Piscataway and branches in Newark and Camden. Rutgers College, located on the College Avenue campus in New Brunswick, is the lineal descendent of Queens College. The name "Queens" was dropped as unpatriotic in 1825, and ties to the Dutch Reformed Church were severed in 1865.

☞ 62 Stevens Institute of Technology
When William Bayard, owner of Castle Point in Hoboken, turned Loyalist late in the American Revolution, he paved the way for engineer and inventor John Stevens to acquire his estate after the war. The talented Stevens and his similarly talented sons contributed much to American technology. They also founded Stevens Institute of Technology in 1870, one of the leading engineering schools in the country.

☞ 63 Moorestown
Moorestown, a Quaker community in Burlington County, is well known for its prestigious Friends School, dating from 1785, and its Friends Meeting House, dating from 1802. The school occupies an attractive campus off West Main Street in the center of town.

☞ 64 Cathedral of the Sacred Heart
This is a truly monumental Roman Catholic church. Construction on it began in 1899 and was finished in 1954. Noted for its 200 stained-glass windows, it is also reputedly the first cathedral in the United States to have its own symphony orchestra. The Cathedral of the Sacred Heart is located east of Branch Brook Park at 89 Ridge Street, Newark.

☞ 65 Cherry Hill East and West High Schools, Haddonfield Memorial High School

Cherry Hill East High School ranks near the top among New Jersey high schools having the highest average SAT scores and the highest percentage of students winning academic awards. In 1991 the school had 24 National Merit Scholarship semifinalists. Haddonfield Memorial High School sends a very large percentage of its students on to college. In the *New Jersey Monthly* article, "Top 75 Public High Schools" (September 1994), Cherry Hill West High School also makes the list.

☞ 66 Princeton University

The College of New Jersey opened at Elizabeth in 1747, its aim being to fill the need for Presbyterian educators. Its original faculty consisted of one man, Jonathan Dickinson, who served as the first president. The second president of the college was Aaron Burr, father of the third U.S. Vice President. In 1756 the college moved to the newly completed Nassau Hall in Princeton. Not until 1896, however, on the 150th anniversary of the chartering of the institution, did the name officially change to Princeton University. It is New Jersey's only Ivy League school.

☞ 67 Dwight-Englewood School

New Jersey has several outstanding preparatory schools, of which Dwight-Englewood is one. Located in Englewood on the corner of North Woodlawn and Palisade Avenues, it is a day school enrolling boys and girls in grades 7 through 12. Private schools, more than public schools, seem to showcase their famous graduates, and Dwight-Englewood definitely has some.

☞ 68 University High School, Science High School

Just as New York City has its Stuyvesant High School and its Bronx High School of Science, so does Newark have a couple of high schools for students with special academic interests. University High School, at 55 Clinton Place, has about 400 students in grades 7 through 12. Science High School, at 40 Rector Street, has 480 or so students in grades 9 through 12. Both rank high on the list of New Jersey public high schools sending the highest percentage of graduates to four-year colleges.

☞ 69   First Presbyterian Church, "Old First"
This superb example of Colonial Georgian architecture stands at 820 Broad Street in the heart of Newark's business district. Construction of the church began in 1787, and the present building was dedicated four years later. The stone for it was quarried on Bloomfield Avenue. "Old First" is the direct descendant of a church established by the Puritan Congregationalist founders of Newark. Until 1986 the church owned the valuable land across from it on Broad Street, where the earliest church buildings stood.

☞ 70   Lawrenceville School
An independent preparatory school, coeducational since 1987, Lawrenceville School was founded in 1810 by the Reverend Isaac Van Arsdale Brown, a Presbyterian. The community of Lawrenceville had been known since the 1660s as Maidenhead. As a consequence, Brown's school was at first called the Academy of Maidenhead. Brown took the lead in 1816 in having the name of town and school changed to Lawrenceville, partly for reasons of delicacy, but also to honor James Lawrence, the naval hero in the War of 1812.

Answers Q71 to Q80 / Sports

☞ 71   Jersey Joe Walcott
On July 18, 1951, Jersey Joe Walcott captured the world's heavyweight boxing title by knocking out Ezzard Charles in the seventh round at Pittsburgh. Walcott, born Arnold Cream in 1914, held the title for a year and two months, losing on a 13th-round KO to Rocky Marciano in Philadelphia on September 23, 1952. In retirement, Jersey Joe Walcott was active with youth groups in the Camden area and served as the county sheriff for many years.

☞ 72   Elysian Fields
This first organized baseball game got very little publicity at the time—so little, in fact, that for decades it was assumed that the first such contest had occurred months later, on June 19, 1846, rather than on its actual date of October 21, 1845. But there is

no doubt about the game having been played at the Elysian Fields in Hoboken. The New Yorkers, already called the Knickerbockers, easily defeated the Brooklyn ball club. The Brooklynites were mostly cricketeers from that city's Union Star Cricket Club.

☞ 73 Bill Bradley

Bill Bradley, born in 1943 in Crystal City, Missouri, first came to the attention of New Jerseyans as a Princeton University basketball star. A Rhodes Scholar, he took up professional basketball after college, playing for the New York Knicks from 1967 to 1977. Upon retirement from the game, he moved to Denville and announced his candidacy for the U.S. Senate. First elected in 1979, Bradley, a Democrat, survived a near defeat at the hands of Christine Todd Whitman in 1990.

☞ 74 Althea Gibson

Born in 1927 in Silver, South Carolina, Althea Gibson was one of the superstars of U.S. tennis for a decade. She won ten straight national black women's singles titles, starting in 1948. She broke the color barrier for black athletes at Forest Hills in 1950 and Wimbledon in 1951. In 1957 she won both the U.S. and English singles championships. She repeated in 1958 and then retired. A resident of East Orange, she was named to the National Lawn Tennis Hall of Fame in 1971.

☞ 75 Monte Irvin

One of the country's finest all-around athletes, Monte Irvin was the choice of many Negro League owners to be the player to break the color barrier in major league baseball, but Branch Rickey picked Jackie Robinson instead. Irvin, a graduate of Orange High School and a star for the Newark Eagles, joined the New York Giants in 1949 and two years later led the National League in RBIs with 121. He is in baseball's Hall of Fame.

☞ 76 Jersey City

On Saturday, July 2, 1921, a huge crowed filled the arena at Boyle's Thirty Acres in Jersey City for a heavily promoted heavyweight title fight. The promoter was the flamboyant Tex Rickard; the champion was Jack Dempsey at 188 pounds; the challenger was Georges Carpentier at 172 pounds. At first the Jersey City crowd cheered lustily for the French boxer, but Jack Dempsey won by a knockout in the fourth round.

☞ 77 Vince Lombardi

A native of New York City, Vince Lombardi (1913-70) compiled a brilliant record as head football coach at St. Cecilia's High School in Englewood. Moving up to Fordham and then Army, he continued his success, using primarily the T-formation. In the pro ranks, with the New York Giants and Green Bay Packers, he did equally well. His pro career record as head coach was 105-35-6, a .740 winning percentage, highest of all time.

☞ 78 Jackie Robinson's debut

Jackie Robinson (1919-72) was born in Cairo, Georgia, and grew up in Pasadena, California. He starred in four sports at UCLA—baseball, football, basketball, and track. Following Robinson's discharge from the army after World War II, Brooklyn Dodgers president Branch Rickey signed him to a Montreal Royals' contract. His first game in Triple-A broke the color barrier that had been in place in organized baseball since the 1880s. In this historic game at Roosevelt Stadium, Robinson went four-for-five.

☞ 79 Milt Campbell

Milt Campbell, born in 1933, was an extraordinary athlete at Plainfield High School, scoring 23 touchdowns as a football tailback and establishing New Jersey high school records in three track and field events. After his silver and gold medal performances in the decathlon in 1952 and 1956, Campbell played pro football for one season, 1957, with the Cleveland Browns. A resident of Plainfield, he has operated programs for underprivileged children and lectured widely.

☞ 80 1937, Newark

It isn't easy to pick the best minor league baseball team of all time, but one that draws a good many votes is Jacob Ruppert's 1937 Newark Bears. As author Ronald A. Mayer subtitled his book *The 1937 Newark Bears*, this International League ball club was truly *A Baseball Legend*, winning 109 games and losing only 43. The Bears went on to win the Little World Series against the Columbus Red Birds. Outfielder Charlie Keller was the brightest star, but the team had many other future major leaguers, including Joe Gordon, Babe Dahlgren, George McQuinn, Spud Chandler, Atley Donald, Willard Hershberger, and Buddy Rosar.

Answers ☞81 to ☞90 / Superlatives

☞ 81   Newark, Elizabeth
Newark, with 275,221 people in 1990, is easily New Jersey's largest city. Elizabeth, number four, is the county seat of Union County, the last of New Jersey's 21 counties to be created. With 100,002 people in 1990, it stands just above Woodbridge Township in population size among the state's municipalities. Although New Jersey is the nation's most densely populated state, only Newark and Jersey City rank among the top 100 U.S. cities in population. Newark is number 56; Jersey City is number 67.

☞ 82   All three
Interestingly, all three of New Jersey's tallest buildings are in Jersey City. The 101 Hudson building is 550 feet high. The state's second tallest building, Newport Tower, rises 524 feet, and the third tallest, Exchange Place Centre, is 495 feet. For some reason, the 1995 *World Almanac* ignores Jersey City but lists eight tall buildings in Newark, with the National Newark & Essex Building topping the list at 465 feet.

☞ 83   Suzette Charles
Both Miss Americas from the Garden State have had unusual reigns. Bette Cooper, a shy girl who never expected to win, refused to serve. Suzette Charles won only because the judges' first choice, Vanessa Williams, Miss New York, was found (after winning and being installed) to have posed for photographs that pageant officials deemed embarrassing. Suzette Charles, the first runner-up, stepped in to replace her.

☛ 84 Traffic circle

Back in 1925 traffic circles seemed like a good idea. In the era of the Model T, with light traffic, at least by today's standards, drivers could save time by chugging into the circles and angling off at the desired exit. But, as time went by, heavier traffic and higher-speed automobiles made the circles a nightmare. Adding traffic lights just before the circles has had some effect, but for the busiest traffic circles the only solution has been costly redesign and reconstruction.

☛ 85 High Point State Park

This park comprises more than 13,000 acres in the Kittatinny Mountains, a gift in 1923 of Colonel and Mrs. Anthony R. Kuser of Bernardsville. A monument marks the highest point in the state—1,803 feet above sea level. From the monument visitors can see vistas of New Jersey, New York, and Pennsylvania. A section of the Appalachian Trail goes through the park.

☛ 86 Atlantic City

It could have been called "Boardman's Walk." There are various stories of how Atlantic's City boardwalk originated. One is that hotel owner Jacob Keim became annoyed by guests tracking sand on the carpets of his Chester House hotel. He talked it over with Alex Boardman, a conductor on the Camden and Atlantic railroad. *Voila!* A boardwalk was built, the first one eight feet wide and resting directly on the sand. There have been several since. The present one is 60 feet wide, five miles long, and stands on a steel and concrete foundation.

☛ 87 Tropicana Casino and Resort

Atlantic City casino hotels continue to expand. As of now, the Tropicana Casino and Resort tops all others with 1,624 rooms. However, the Trump Taj Mahal, like the Tropicana (previously TropWorld), is being expanded and may in time become number one. Bally's Park Place, once in first place, will then rank third.

☛ 88 Lake Hopatcong

New Jersey's largest lake was a fashionable resort in the late 19th century. Vacationers traveled by train or steamboat, depending on their destination along the lake. Some of the largest hotels stood at Nolan's Point and Mount Arlington. Particularly imposing was the Mount Arlington's Hotel Breslin, a four-story, 300-room resort hotel that opened in 1887. Rooms rented at $5 a day or $28 a week. The resort hotels on Lake Hopatcong are gone, but tourism on a more modest scale continues. Hopatcong State Park, on the southwestern shore of the lake, offers swimming and picnicking.

☞ 89 Alpine
High atop the Palisades, 530 feet above the Hudson River, is the small community of Alpine, an exclusive place with personal income and property values in the stratosphere. At one time or another it has been home to actor Eddie Murphy, rock-blues singer Stevie Wonder, and mystery writer Donald E. Westlake. The earliest mansions in the area, built along the Palisades after the Civil War, fell victim to the park and the interstate parkway.

☞ 90 Rutgers
Not much travel was required for this first intercollegiate football game, played at New Brunswick on November 6, 1869. Rutgers won by the score of 6-4. The game did not resemble modern football: Each team put 25 men on the field at a time, and the contest was a slapdash affair between gentlemen amateurs.

Answers Q91-100 / The Arts

☞ 91 F. Scott Fitzgerald
A native of St. Paul, Minnesota, Francis Scott Key Fitzgerald (1896-1940) entered Princeton University in 1913, where he became a leader in theatrical and literary activities but left before graduation. While serving in the army during World War I, he met and married Zelda Sayre and wrote *This Side of Paradise,* a novel that defined the jazz age and made him, at age 24, a spokesman for the "lost generation." Fitzgerald's 1925 novel *The Great Gatsby* is considered his masterpiece.

☞ 92 Hoboken

"I coulda had class," Marlon Brando says in the movie *On the Waterfront*. "I coulda been a contender." Actually, the mumbling method actor did have class at that stage of his career, and he won the 1954 Academy Award for Best Actor. The movie garnered seven other Oscars as well, including the one for Best Picture. Filmed on the Hoboken docks, it is a devastating look at union racketeering on the New York-New Jersey waterfront.

☞ 93 Michael Graves

Architect Michael Graves, born in 1934, stands at the very top of his profession. Among the buildings that this Indianapolis-born, Princeton-based architect has designed are the Portland Building in Portland, Oregon, and the Walt Disney Company corporate headquarters in Burbank, California. He designed the renovations for the Newark Museum on Washington Street, Newark, and the Whitney Museum of American Art in New York City. Michael Graves is noted, too, for his furniture designs.

☞ 94 Thomas Nast

Thomas Nast (1840-1902), caricaturist, illustrator, and painter, was born in Landau, Germany. He came to the United States as a child. His early work for *Frank Leslie's Illustrated Newspaper* and *Harper's Weekly* attracted wide attention, especially his cartoons of the American Civil War. His home on Macculloch Avenue, Morristown, is a private residence with a plaque honoring Nast. In addition to originating the GOP elephant, the Democratic donkey, and the Tammany tiger, Thomas Nast created the familiar image of Uncle Sam.

☞ 95 *The Perils of Pauline*

This famous 1914 serial concerns Pauline's hairbreadth escapes from the attempts on her life by a thoroughly contemptible guardian. Directed by Donald Mackenzie, the Fort Lee serial co-stars Pearl White and Crane Wilbur. Later attempts to capitalize on this classic title include a 1947 movie starring Betty Hutton that masquerades as a biography of Pearl White and a 1967 expanded TV pilot with Pat Boone and Pamela Austin that has nothing to do with Pearl or the Palisades.

☞ 96 Judy Blume

Born Judy Sussman in Elizabeth in 1938, Judy Blume has written
a succession of popular, realistic novels for preteens and teenagers. Among her best-known works are *Blubber* and *Tales of a
Fourth Grade Nothing* for younger readers and *Hello, God, It's
Me, Margaret* and *Tiger Eyes* for young adults. Her approach is
direct, sympathetic, and psychologically on target.

☞ 97 William Carlos Williams

One of America's greatest poets, William Carlos Williams (1883-
1963) was born in Rutherford and practiced medicine there for 40
years. In his poems he uses idiomatic speech and details of
commonplace experiences. His best-known work is undoubtedly
Paterson, a sprawling five-volume poem containing a great deal of
quoted prose. It concerns the appearance, history, and surround-
ings of its title city.

☞ 98 George Segal

A member of the pop art movement, sculptor George Segal, born
in New York City in 1924, began as a realist painter. Today he is
well known for his tableaux of white-plaster figures cast from
live models. The figures are generally melancholy, portraying the
alienation of modern life. His work can be seen in the garden at
the Newark Museum and in New York City's Museum of Modern
Art. Segal makes his home in South Brunswick.

☞ 99 Stephen Crane

Stephen Crane (1871-1900) was a novelist, a short story writer, a
poet, and a newspaper reporter—all in the span of his 28 years.
Born at 14 Mulberry Place in Newark, he lived as a child in
Asbury Park. Crane's literary reputation was established in 1895
with the publication of *The Red Badge of Courage,* a novel about
the Civil War. His short story, "The Open Boat," is also widely
known and often anthologized.

☞ 100 Paper Mill Playhouse

The Paper Mill Playhouse has the largest subscription base and
the greatest earned income of any regional theater in the United
States. Its productions can be as lavish as Broadway's, and the

stars who have performed here are legion. They include Colleen Dewhurst, Tony Randall, and Jason Robards, Jr. Many of the plays at the Paper Mill are revivals, but not all of them. New plays open here as well.

PAULINE
+
PALISADES
—
PERIL!

The motion picture industry began in Fort Lee, migrated west to Tinseltown, and in recent years has been returning (now and then) to the general area of Pauline's peril. A key scene in the 1982 film *Tootsie* was shot in Fort Lee's Plaza West Shopping Center.

Answers ✿1 to ✿10 / Entertainers

✿ 1 Sterling Hayden

Born Sterling Walter Relyea in Montclair, actor Sterling Hayden (1916-86) made his film debut in 1941 in the movie *Virginia,* with Madeleine Carroll and Fred MacMurray. He appeared in a succession of movies in the 1950s, after which his acting took second place to his part-time exploring, as described in *Wanderer.* One of his later film efforts is in *9 to 5,* in which the stars are three savvy secretaries, played by Jane Fonda, Lily Tomlin, and Dolly Parton.

✿ 2 Annie Oakley

The inspiration for Irving Berlin's musical *Annie Get Your Gun* was born in Darke County, Ohio, in 1860. She married Frank E. Butler, a professional marksman and vaudeville star, after defeating him in a marksmanship contest. Annie Oakley was a star attraction in Buffalo Bill's Wild West Show from 1885 to 1902, performing remarkable feats of target shooting. In December 1893 she and her husband moved into a house built for them on Grant Avenue in Nutley. She died in 1926.

✿ 3 Ray Liotta

Ray Liotta, born in Newark in 1955, enjoyed a rapid rise to stardom following his well-reviewed debut in the 1986 film *Something Wild,* with Jeff Daniels and Melanie Griffith. After gaining widespread notice in his leading role as a mobster-turned-informant in *GoodFellas,* Liotta went on to play other leading roles in such films as *Unlawful Entry* and *Operation Dumbo Drop.*

✿ 4 Susan Sarandon

Born Susan Abigail Tomaling in 1946 in New York City, actress Susan Sarandon was one of nine children. She grew up in Edison and graduated from Edison High School. Her marriage to actor Chris Sarandon ended in divorce. She was nominated for an Academy Award for her role in *Thelma & Louise,* and was nominated again three years later for her portrayal of a tough, principled lawyer in *The Client.*

✿ 5 Count Basie

William Basie (1904-84), born in Red Bank, was given the nickname "Count" early in his career as a disk jockey. An accomplished pianist, Basie joined Benny Moten's Kansas City Orchestra in 1929. In 1935 he formed his own band, later enlarged, which moved to New York City. By the end of the 1930s the Count Basie Orchestra was world famous. A major figure in the "swing" era of jazz, he introduced many outstanding soloists, including saxophonist Lester Young and trumpet player Buck Clayton.

✿ 6 Lotta Crabtree

Commonly called "Miss Lotta," the actress Lotta Crabtree (1847-1924) was known as "the nation's darling" at the height of her career. Born in New York City, she achieved fame in California as a child for her singing, dancing, and reciting. She returned in triumph to New York in the late 1860s. A pert comedienne, she never married. Her mother built an 18-room summer "cottage" for her in 1885-86 on Edgemere Avenue in Mount Arlington.

✿ 7 Jerome Kern

Jerome Kern (1885-1945) is one of America's best known songwriters. Born in New York City, he studied in New York and New Jersey. His greatest triumph was the 1927 musical *Show Boat* and its classic song "Ol' Man River." Kern later won Oscars for the songs "The Way You Look Tonight" and "The Last Time I Saw Paris."

✿ 8 Linda Hunt

Not to be confused with the glamorous Helen Hunt, character actress Linda Hunt was born in Morristown in 1945. A stage actress prior to her 1983 Academy Award winning performance as Best Supporting Actress in the Australian film *The Year of Living Dangerously*, she has since appeared in other movies, including *Waiting for the Moon*, playing the part of Alice B. Toklas.

✿ 9 Frankie Valli

From 1962 to 1970 The Four Seasons recorded 29 songs that made the charts. Their leader, vocalist Frankie Valli, was born in Newark in 1937. Other members of the group also hailed from New Jersey, including Tommy De Vito from Belleville and Nick Massi from Newark. Among the group's many hits were "Rag Doll" and "Can't Take My Eyes off of You."

✿ 10 Dionne Warwick

Born Marie Warrick in East Orange in 1940, Dionne Warwick sang as a child with the Drinkard Singers at the New Hope Baptist Church in Newark before moving on to commercial success. Her smooth and distinctive voice won her a large following. Among her best-known recordings are "That's What Friends Are For" and "Do You Know the Way to San Jose?" for which San Jose named her an honorary citizen.

Answers ✿11 to ✿20 / Movers and Shakers

✿ 11 Garret A. Hobart

"Rarely has an American Vice President brought to the office ability as great as that of Garret A. Hobart." This quote comes from a glowing sidebar in the American Heritage history of U.S. Presidents. Hobart, a Long Branch native who practiced law in Paterson, entered the New Jersey legislature in 1872 and over time became one of the leading Republicans in New Jersey. He was nominated for Vice President in 1896 to help William McKinley carry the then-traditionally Democratic state. The strategy worked.

✿ 12 Effa Manley

Wife of Abe Manley and co-owner with him of the Newark Eagles of the Negro National League, Effa Manley (1900-81) was a shrewd and dynamic executive. Among the great black players who starred for the Manleys' ball club were Larry Doby, Monte Irvin, and Don Newcombe. Mrs. Manley was furious when major league owners began signing away these outstanding players in the late 1940s, but there was little she could do about it. The Newark Eagles disbanded in 1948.

✿ 13 Antonin Scalia
Born in 1936 in Trenton, Antonin Scalia moved with his family to Elmhurst, Queens, as a young boy. After graduating from Harvard Law School, he taught law at the University of Virginia and the University of Chicago. In 1982 Scalia became a federal judge in the District of Columbia. Four years later President Ronald Reagan nominated him for the U.S. Supreme Court. An outspoken conservative, Scalia has helped to tilt the court toward the right.

✿ 14 Hetty Green
Inheriting a large fortune from her father, Hetty Green (1836-1916), a native of New Bedford, Massachusetts, managed it with notable skill and parsimony. She became generally known as the greatest woman financier in the world. She was also one of the cheapest. On a January day in 1906, when Hetty Green lacked the needed five-cent streetcar fare in Hoboken, the conductor paid it for her.

✿ 15 A. Harry Moore
For much of New Jersey's history, its governors could hold office more than once but not consecutively. A. Harry Moore (1879-1952) was governor in 1926-29, 1932-35, and 1938-41. Hudson County's political machine dominated New Jersey politics during that period, and it is therefore not surprising that Moore, a Democrat, came from Jersey City.

✿ 16 Millicent Fenwick
A patrician Republican who inspired cartoonist Garry Trudeau's Lacey Davenport in "Doonesbury," Millicent Fenwick (1910-92) was first elected to Congress at the age of 64. Prior to that, she worked for many years as a writer and editor for *Vogue* magazine. Fenwick, a resident of Bernardsville, also served in the New Jersey General Assembly and in the Division of Consumer Affairs before winning her seat in Congress.

✿ 17 Seth Boyden
Seth Boyden (1788-1870), New Jersey's "Uncommercial Inventor," was born in Foxboro, Massachusetts, but spent 55 years in or

near Newark. The developer of patent leather and malleable iron, he never made money off his innovations, and he died in poverty. In his later years Seth Boyden lived on a farm near Maplewood, where he perfected the huge Hilton strawberry.

✿ 18 Elizabeth Haddon

John Haddon, an English Quaker, sent his young, unmarried daughter, Elizabeth Haddon (1680-1762), overseas to develop a 500-acre plantation he had purchased in New Jersey. Showing indomitable spirit, she did it. Later, when the man she loved, John Estaugh, hesitated to declare his intentions, Elizabeth prompted him to propose, a story told in Longfellow's *Tales of a Wayside Inn.* Haddonfield is named after Elizabeth Haddon.

✿ 19 Frank Hague

For four decades Frank Hague (1876-1956), a big-city political boss, held sway in Jersey City, in Hudson County, and often in the entire state. A machine Democrat, he had worked his way up through the ranks, taking over as mayor of Jersey City in 1917 and holding the office through 1947. The 1949 elections cost him much of his power—power that at one unguarded moment had led him to say, "I am the law in Jersey City."

✿ 20 James H. Birch

Known as the wagonmaker to the world, James H. Birch (1829-1927) began his business at the corner of Broad and Liberty Streets in Burlington in 1862. The Civil War was a good time for wagonmakers, and Birch prospered. His plant expanded to 15 acres, his models grew to about 200, and his yearly shipments went as high as 10,000. The horseless carriage doomed the wagon industry, and Birch's plant closed after World War I.

Answers ✿21 to ✿30 / Events

✿ 21 New Brunswick

The male victim, shot once, was the Reverend Edward W. Hall, rector of the Church of St. John the Evangelist in New Brunswick.

The female victim, shot three times and her throat cut, was Mrs. Eleanor Mills, a choir singer at Saint John's. Their bodies were found in a secluded lovers' lane, just off De Russey's Lane, about 350 feet into Somerset County. Three people were tried for the crime—the rector's widow, Mrs. Frances Hall, and her two brothers. All were acquitted.

✿ 22 A leap over the Passaic Falls

Sam Patch had a ready-made crowd. People had gathered to watch the building of a bridge over the Passaic River at the Great Falls. Instead they saw a daredevil in action. Despite attempts to stop him, young Sam Patch leapt over the 70-foot waterfall and into the river. Patch, a cotton mill worker in Passaic, made headlines with his feat. Next summer in New York State he tried a 100-foot Niagara leap, and survived. A few months after that, he tried a 125-foot leap at Genesee Falls, and died.

✿ 23 Clara Maass

In 1901 the U.S. army was conducting experiments in Cuba to see if a bite from a diseased mosquito could, if carefully monitored, immunize the person bitten from yellow fever. Two volunteers had already died. Clara Maass, 25, a contract nurse from East Orange, took the risk, trying for the sixth time to gain the immunity that would allow her to work among yellow fever victims. Four days later her temperature began to climb, and on the tenth day she died.

✿ 24 World War I

Anti-German feeling in World War I prompted the people of Newark to rename several streets that bore German names. During the war, German Valley in Morris County became Long Valley, and New Germantown in Hunterdon County became Oldwick. This semantic commotion occurred elsewhere, too. Some people began calling sauerkraut "victory cabbage."

✿ 25 Cable-car principle

Joseph Francis (1801-93), a native of Boston who lived in Toms River, had a lifetime interest in unsinkable boats and in life-saving devices generally. He adapted an open-bucket design that another Ocean County inventor, Dr. William A. Newell of Mana-hawkin, had developed a year earlier. Francis's watertight life car, used in the 1850 *Ayrshire* rescue off Manasquan, was a ship-to-shore cable-car system that carried people to safety from wrecked ships that lay just offshore.

✿ 26 Greenwich
This small Cumberland County community made news on Decem-ber 22, 1774, when a group of angry citizens, disguised as Indians, marched from nearby Shiloh to Greenwich and burned a British cargo of tea. The tea had been stored for ten days in the cellar of a local merchant. Seven of the tea burners were brought to trial. All were acquitted. One of them, Richard Howell, was later elected governor of New Jersey.

✿ 27 Dutch Schultz
Arthur Flegenheimer reportedly took the name Dutch Schultz because "it was short enough to fit in the headlines." And Schultz often made the headlines during the chaotic beer wars of the early 1930s. When the Dutchman took a notion to kill New York special prosecutor Thomas E. Dewey, clearer syndicate heads prevailed. They decided to kill Schultz instead, which they did on the evening of October 23, 1935, at the Palace Chop House and Tavern, 12 East Park Street, Newark.

✿ 28 Jersey Devil
Sometimes called the Leeds Devil, since he/she/it was reputedly born to one Mrs. Leeds of Estelville in 1887, the Devil has reappeared—or been reported to reappear—in many southern New Jersey communities in the 20th century, among them Trenton in 1909 and Batsto and Woodstown in 1936. Descrip-tions of the Jersey Devil vary, but most agree on the creature's cloven hoofs and batlike wings. New Jersey's hockey team is named after the creature.

✿ 29 George B. McClellan
He was never the "Young Napoleon" that Northerners wanted him to be. But George Brinton McClellan (1826-85) was an able, if overcautious, general who halted Robert E. Lee's first invasion

of the North at the Battle of Antietam. Relieved of command for his failure to pursue Lee, "Little Mac" ran for President against Lincoln in 1864 and lost. Later, as a resident of West Orange, he was chosen by the Democrats to run for governor of New Jersey. He won, serving from 1878 to 1881.

✿ 30 Woodbridge
This commuter train, *The Broker*, was carrying more than its usual number of homeward-bound passengers from New York due to a Jersey Central strike. As its name implies, many of the commuters were well-to-do professionals. On a temporary wooden bridge at Woodbridge, built because of highway construction, the train derailed.

Answers ✿31 to ✿40 / Buildings

✿ 31 Emlen Physick House
There are a great many carefully restored and maintained Victorian houses in Cape May, but the Emlen Physick House is the city's showplace. An 18-room mansion designed by noted architect Frank Furness on an eight-acre estate, it was built in 1881 for Emlen Physick, the grandson of Philip Physick, a Philadelphia physician who is sometimes called the "father of surgery." It is now both a museum and the headquarters of the Mid-Atlantic Center for the Arts.

✿ 32 Stockton Inn
Stockton got its start as a Delaware River ferry town in the early 18th century. What is now Colligan's Stockton Inn was built back then as a private home. It dates to around 1710. In the early 19th century it was converted to an inn. A hundred years later Richard Rodgers and Lorenz Hart wrote the song about it, containing the lines, "There's a small hotel, with a wishing well."

✿ 33 Elias Boudinot
Surely one of the least-known founders of the nation, Elias Boudinot (1740-1821) owned Boxwood Hall in Elizabeth at the

time of the American Revolution. As president of the Continental Congress, Boudinot signed the peace treaty with Great Britain. In 1789, as a Congressman, he asked President Washington to proclaim a national day of Thanksgiving, which Washington did. Boudinot served as director of the U.S. Mint from 1795 to 1805. He sold Boxwood Hall to Senator Jonathan Dayton, a prominent New Jerseyan who later moved on to help develop Dayton, Ohio.

✿ 34 Cape May

In the 1840s and '50s Cape May was the nation's leading seaside resort, visited by Southern planters, Northern socialites, and Washington politicians. Large seaside hotels were built, including the immense Mount Vernon. These frame stuctures were extremely vulnerable to fire. The Mount Vernon went up in smoke in 1856. Fire destroyed a quarter of the Cape May business district in 1869, including several hotels. Then on November 9, 1878, flames swept through the heart of the city, causing devastating losses.

✿ 35 Frelinghuysen Arboretum

The striking white mansion, once the home of George Griswold and Sarah Ballantine Frelinghuysen, now houses the administrative offices of the Morris County Park Commission. The rest of the 127-acre estate, open to the public, comprises the arboretum, which features natural and formal gardens, labeled collections of trees and shrubs, and a Braille nature trail.

✿ 36 Stage House Inn

Built in 1737 or thereabouts, the Stage House Inn in Scotch Plains served as a stagecoach stop from about 1769 to 1829. The inn has become the anchor for Stage House Village, a group of older buildings, some from other sites, that house various shops and other restaurants.

✿ 37 Ringwood Manor

A national historic landmark, Ringwood Manor, located in Passaic County near the New York State line, owes its existence to the iron industry. An early resident, Robert Erskine, was surveyor general to the Continental army. A later ironmaster, Martin Ryerson, was succeeded by Peter Cooper (founder of New York's Cooper Union), and by industrialist Abram S. Hewitt.

✿ 38 Marlpit Hall

The Monmouth County Historical Association maintains and operates four historic houses in the county. The other three are the Allen House in Shrewsbury, the Covenhoven House in Free-hold, and the Holmes-Hendrickson House in Holmdel. This one, Marlpit Hall, at 137 Kings Highway, Middletown, was enlarged by Tory merchant John Taylor around 1740 and remained in the Taylor family for nearly 100 years. Acquired in 1936, it has been furnished to show how styles and tastes have changed over the generations. Major revovation of historic Marlpit Hall began in 1995.

✿ 39 High Point Inn

Standing on a hilltop overlooking Lake Marcia in what is now High Point State Park, the High Point Inn, built in 1888 by Charles St. John, commanded a spectacular view of the country-side, luring wealthy weekenders from New York and Philadelphia. Soon after the turn of the century fire gutted the building. Anthony Kuser of Bernardsville inherited the property and in 1911 built a stately summer home on the site of the old inn. In time the Kusers donated their 40-room mansion and 11,000 acres of land to the State of New Jersey. After many years of failing to maintain the mansion properly, the state decided to demolish it.

✿ 40 Georgian Court College

George Jay Gould, son of financier Jay Gould, commissioned architect Bruce Price, designer of the Chateau Frontenac in Quebec and Tuxedo Park in New York State, to plan and build an estate in Lakewood. Price wrought well. Four of the original buildings remain—a mansion, a casino, a stable, and what is now the chaplain's house. In 1924 the Sisters of Mercy purchased the estate, which provided an elegant and ready-made campus for Georgian Court College, founded in 1908 and serving about 2,500 students.

Answers ✿41 to ✿50 / Businesses

✿ 41 Montvale

A pioneering effort in the chain-store concept, the Great Atlantic & Pacific Tea Company, founded in 1869 by George Huntington Hartford, expanded rapidly, undersold its competition, and prospered mightily for a hundred years. Hartford cloned his original store on Vesey Street, New York City, into thousands of similar stores. After hard times in the 1970s, A&P bounced back under German ownership. In 1992 the company employed 15,000 workers in New Jersey and nearly 100,000 worldwide.

✿ 42 Mars, Inc. (M&M/Mars Division)

Founded by Forrest E. Mars, Sr., in a one-room apartment over a candy factory in Minneapolis, the company moved to a plant in Chicago when its Milky Way candy bar proved a big hit with the public. Now headquartered in McLean, Virginia, Mars, Inc., has 15 factories in the United States, 41 worldwide, and produces a variety of products, including M&Ms, Mars, DoveBars, Twix, Kudos, Rondos, Uncle Ben's Rice, and its best-selling candy bar, Snickers.

✿ 43 The Manor

New Jersey has more than its share of fine restaurants, places where both the food and the ambiance are first class. The Manor, at 111 Prospect Avenue, West Orange, is one of them. Consistently earning high ratings from all reviewers, The Manor, featuring a lobster buffet from Tuesday through Saturday, is huge and opulent, seating 350 in its plush French Regency dining room plus 1,300 in catering. The formal grounds are impressive.

✿ 44 Fair Lawn

Thousands of New Jersey schoolchildren have trooped through the Nabisco Fair Lawn Bakery at 2211 Route 208, watching the production of Oreos, Chips Ahoy, and other famous-name cookies and crackers. Although RJR Nabisco is headquartered in New York, Nabisco, Inc., which is to say the nontobacco part of the business, is a major New Jersey employer.

✿ 45   Paterson

The 77-foot-high Great Falls of the Passaic River were an early tourist attraction. During the Revolution, Alexander Hamilton visited the area and saw the industrial potential in harnessing the power of the falls. Twelve years later, as Secretary of the Treasury, Hamilton arranged private support for establishing a planned industrial city. The place was named Paterson in honor of the man who was then governor of the state. Hamilton's plan succeeded, and Paterson became a leading industrial city.

✿ 46   Roebling

Roebling is located on the Delaware River a few miles south of Trenton. The town was laid out by Charles G. Roebling, one of the three sons of John Roebling, the founder of a cable manufacturing company in Trenton. A pioneer in building suspension bridges, the elder Roebling built the Allegheny Suspension Bridge at Pittsburgh in 1845 and was working on the Brooklyn Bridge at the time of his death. The town of Roebling originally consisted of brick row houses for the workers and more spacious homes for the higher-ups.

✿ 47   Renault Winery

Egg Harbor City was settled by Germans, but it was a Frenchman, Louis N. Renault, who made it big in the wine business. The Renault Winery has been in operation continuously since the 1870s when the founder established his business in this area already noted for its grapes and winemaking. At one time Renault, located at 72 North Bremen Avenue, was the nation's largest champagne producer.

✿ 48   Pharmaceutical industry

Although Johnson & Johnson and Merck & Company are the giants among New Jersey pharmaceutical companies, all of those listed in the question are major corporations. Schering-Plough is headquartered in Madison, Warner-Lambert in Morris Plains, and Becton, Dickinson in Franklin Lakes. Large foreign-based pharmaceutical companies also have headquarters in New Jersey, including CIBA-GEIGY in Freehold and Hoffman-LaRoche in Clifton.

✿ 49 "Trenton Makes—The World Takes"

In the 1920s and '30s no one could question the accuracy of this proud motto above the Lower Trenton Bridge across the Delaware River. In the 1930s more than 120,000 people lived in Trenton, producing an array of products in steel, rubber, and ceramics. The city was well known for its cigars, parachutes, canned goods, and Lenox china. Today, with a population of approximately 88,000, the capital city of New Jersey is again experiencing business and industrial growth.

✿ 50 Toys 'R' Us

This toy-supermarket chain is one of the great success stories of modern retailing. Founded in Washington, D.C., by Charles Lazarus in 1948, it took its present name (with the *R* written backwards) in 1957. Headquartered in Paramus, by 1990 it was operating more than 400 toy stores worldwide.

Answers ✿51 to ✿60 / Places

✿ 51 Dingmans Bridge

This bridge, high above the Delaware in northwestern New Jersey, leads to Dingmans Ferry, Pennsylvania. It is something of a throwback to the old days of private toll roads and toll collectors. The steel-and-wood bridge, solid but rustic, is named for Judge David W. Dingman, who lived in the area in Revolutionary times. The toll, which goes to the owners and operators of the bridge, has kept pace with that of the newer government-built bridge to Milford, Pennsylvania, a few miles north.

✿ 52 East Paterson

If you have trouble remembering this particular name change, notice that the old *E.P.* initials are retained in the town's new and more fashionable name, Elmwood Park. Residents who disliked the former name would probably also dislike the Federal Writers Project's dismissal of their Passaic County community in 1939 as "little more than an industrial adjunct to Paterson."

✿ 53 Woodbury

Clearly, the answer to this question will be easy for people who live in Glassboro or Pitman (or in Woodbury itself, of course). Woodbury is a handsome town of about 10,000 near where the Delaware River meets Woodbury Creek. Founded by Quakers, it has been the county seat of Gloucester County since 1785. One of the town's early buildings is the Friends Meeting House on North Broad Street. One of its best-known 19th-century residents was G. G. Green, who made his fortune producing patent medicines. Green had a summer home on Lake Hopatcong.

✿ 54 Named after a type of aquatic mollusk

Bivalves can be oysters, or mussels, or clams. The name comes from the fact that these mollusks have a shell consisting of two valves hinged together. For years the community of Bivalve on the Maurice River in Cumberland County was the center of New Jersey's oyster industry. But in the 1950s a parasite began attacking the oysters, dramatically reducing their numbers. Many of the boats still go out, but the largest yield now is quahog clams—which are also bivalves.

✿ 55 Cranberries

New Jersey is one of the leading states in the nation in the production of cranberries, outranked only by Massachusetts and Wisconsin. New Jersey is *the* leading state in the production of cultivated blueberries. The two are closely related; some experts consider the cranberry to belong to the blueberry genus *Vaccinium.* Early settlers found wild cranberries and blueberries growing in profusion in the Pine Barrens. Cultivation has resulted in two of the state's major cash crops.

✿ 56 Vineland

Vineland, in Cumberland County, was founded in 1861 by Charles K. Landis, a 28-year-old Philadelphia lawyer and banker, who bought 32,000 acres in Millville Township and laid out a mile-square central city, which he called Vineland. The surrounding agricultural area was Landis Township until 1952, when the city and township incorporated as one geographically vast city. Its 1990 population was 54,780.

✿ 57 Bergen County

While it's true that what is now Hudson County was first settled by the Dutch, it's also true that from 1675 until 1840 Hudson County's territory was included in Bergen County. Present-day Bergen County is recognizably Dutch, from its Dutch colonial houses to its Dutch Reformed Churches. The place names, however, are primarily English and Indian. Even the name Hackensack, which sounds vaguely Dutch, is of Indian origin.

✿ 58 Blue uniforms of New Jersey soldiers

New Jersey's troops wore blue uniforms in the French and Indian War. A few years later, in the Revolutionary War, General George Washington decreed that the New Jersey militia wear blue uniforms. Washington specifically designated these units as Jersey Blues. During the Civil War, the name was once again applied to state regiments and to New Jerseyans in general, usually connoting patriotic fervor. The name persisted as a sobriquet for the state after the Civil War ended.

✿ 59 Atlantic City

The 1944 movie *Atlantic City* is more noteworthy for its music than its plot. The orchestras of Paul Whiteman and Louis Armstrong are on hand, along with bug-eyed comic Jerry Colonna and Latina dancer Adele Mara. Considerably more serious is the 1980 *Atlantic City*, a character study of an aging, anachronistically proud, small-time hood, played by Burt Lancaster, in an Atlantic City that is changing from a down-at-the-heels resort to a big-money casino town.

✿ 60 Batsto

Bog iron brought Charles Read of Burlington to the Pine Barrens, where in 1766 he erected an iron furnace on the Mullica River. The village of Batsto grew up around it. During the Revolutionary War and the War of 1812, the Batsto ironworks produced cannons and cannonballs. In peacetime it turned out iron pipe, Dutch ovens, and other items. When better iron ore was found elsewhere, the industry died. So did Batsto, but it has now been restored as a historic museum village. The ironmaster's house is its centerpiece.

Answers ✿61 to ✿70 / Religion and Education

✿ 61 Mount Holly
At 35 Brainerd Street in Mount Holly stands what is probably
New Jersey's oldest surviving schoolhouse. A one-room brick
building that dates to 1759, it is now operated as a museum by
the Colonial Dames of America. The Reverend John Brainerd,
who, like his brother David, was a famed Indian missionary,
taught at the school in 1767.

✿ 62 Seton Hall University and College of Saint Elizabeth
Seton Hall University in South Orange, founded in 1856, has
approximately 4,400 undergraduates and 10,000 students in all.
The College of Saint Elizabeth in Convent Station, founded in
1899 and the first four-year college in New Jersey to grant
baccalaurate degrees to women, is attended by about 1,500
students, 90% of them women. Both are independent Roman
Catholic institutions.

✿ 63 Rutgers Preparatory School
This is the oldest preparatory school in New Jersey, dating from
1766. Enrolling boys and girls in pre-kindergarten through 12th
grade, it has approximately 550 students. The poet Joyce Kilmer
attended Rutgers Prep from 1894 to 1904, went on to Rutgers
University for two years, enlisted in the army in World War I, and
was killed on July 30, 1918, at Château-Thierry in the Second
Battle of the Marne.

✿ 64 Presbyterians
Presbyterianism is essentially a form of Protestant church
organization, favoring a central church government. The main
body of Puritans opted for this organizational plan, and the many
Presbyterian churches in New Jersey reflect their choice. Congregationalists, by contrast, regard the church as an autonomous
group of believers and reject a larger church hierarchy. There are
many more Presbyterian churches than Congregationalist churches
in the state.

✿ 65 Thomas H. Kean

The popular 58th governor of New Jersey served two terms
during the prosperous 1980s and was often mentioned as a
Vice Presidential possibility. He pursued a course of moderate
Republicanism, as shown in his 1988 book, *The Politics of
Inclusion*. When his second term ended, Kean accepted the
presidency of Drew University.

✿ 66 Mountain Lakes High School

Whenever *Star-Ledger* columnist Robert Braun writes about New
Jersey's best public high schools, he usually mentions Mountain
Lakes High School. By any measure, it is academically one of the
finest public high schools in the state. Among the others that
typically come very close on the SAT-average scale are Chatham,
Cherry Hill East, Holmdel, Millburn, Princeton, and Tenafly.

✿ 67 Episcopalians

In the United States the Church of England is the Episcopal
Church, a strong presence in New Jersey since colonial times.
One of the oldest church buildings in New Jersey, dating from
1703, stands at the corner of Wood and West Broad Streets in
Burlington. Built of brick, it is old St. Mary's Episcopal Church.
There is a new St. Mary's, too, built in 1854, with a cemetery
between it and the older church.

✿ 68 Academic High School, Jersey City

This school was cited in a recent issue of *New Jersey Monthly* as
"an example of urban education that works." Prospective students
go through a screening process that includes test scores, teacher
recommendations, and elementary school performance. Academic High, a multicultural school, has a strict dress code for its 400
or so students. The school offers an unusually high percentage of
Advanced Placement courses, and in 1993 sent 96.9% of its
graduates on to four-year colleges.

✿ 69 Quakers

Strictly speaking, the followers of this denomination belong to the
Society of Friends, but early in their history they acquired the
name Quakers, presumably because of founder George Fox's

admonition to "quake" at the word of the Lord. Quakers settled much of southern New Jersey, and their plain meeting houses exist in many towns throughout that region. Nor are they entirely absent from the north. The oldest church building in Morris County is the Friends Meeting House in Randolph.

✿ 70 Reformed Church in America, or Dutch Reformed

Dutch Reformed Churches (now officially the Reformed Church in America) appear most often in the northern and central counties, especially Bergen, Somerset, and Middlesex, where early Dutch settlement occurred. Dutch Reformers were responsible for the founding of Queens College, now Rutgers University. In addition to the Church on the Green in Hackensack, the Old Paramus Reformed Church in Ridgewood and the Old Dutch Parsonage in Somerville are noteworthy Dutch Reformed buildings in the state.

Answers S71-S80 / Sports

✿ 71 Tommy Heinsohn

Tommy Heinsohn first attracted attention as a basketball player at St. Michael's High School in Union City. He went on to star for Holy Cross, averaging 22.1 points a game. A consensus All-American in 1956, the six-foot-seven Heinsohn joined the Boston Celtics, with whom he played from 1957 to 1965. Known for his line-drive hook shot, he was on a championship team every year but one.

✿ 72 Larry Doby

Although he started as an infielder, Paterson's Larry Doby spent most of his 13-year major-league career patrolling the outfield for the Cleveland Indians. In his first full season in the majors, 1948, he batted .301 and helped lead Cleveland to the American League pennant and victory in the World Series. Doby, who made the All-Star team six times, retired in 1960 with a .282 lifetime average. He later joined the office of the Commissioner of Major League Baseball.

☼ 73 Franco Harris

Franco Harris of Mount Holly and Penn State was the Pittsburgh Steelers' first draft choice in 1972. That year he became only the fifth rookie in NFL history to gain more than 1,000 yards. In a late December playoff game between the Steelers and the Oakland Raiders, he made the most dramatic game-winning touchdown in Steeler history, catching a desperately thrown, deflected pass and racing into the end zone for the victory. The catch went down in football history as "The Immaculate Reception."

☼ 74 Atlantic City Bacharach Giants

Through most of the 1920s, shortstop Dick Lundy starred for the Atlantic City Bacharach Giants of the Eastern Colored League. An outstanding fielder and a fine hitter, the graceful Lundy, a native of northern Florida, led his team to pennants in 1926 and 1927. Like "King Richard," as Lundy was sometimes called, John Henry "Pop" Lloyd was also a shortstop for the Bacharach Giants. The Eastern Colored League failed in 1928, but the Bacahrach Giants struggled on for a couple more seasons, 1929 and 1934.

☼ 75 Frederick "Red" Cochrane

One of New Jersey's many outstanding professional boxers, Red Cochrane was born in Elizabeth and, as a youngster, won the New Jersey Golden Gloves lightweight championship. Turning pro, he captured the world welterweight title in 1941 by defeating Fritzie Zivic. He fought two memorable battles against Rocky Graziano at Madison Square Garden. After losing his title in 1946, he retired. A resident of Union, he operated Cochrane's Bar in Hillside for several years.

☼ 76 Amos Alonzo Stagg

Best known as a football coach, Amos Alonzo Stagg was also a superb athlete. Playing end at Yale, he was named to the first All-American football team. In baseball, his pitching won him a bonus offer from the New York Metropolitans. But it was as a football coach at the University of Chicago that Stagg gained his reputation. From 1905 to 1909 his Maroons lost just two games. After mandatory retirement from Chicago, he coached with great success at the College of the Pacific.

✿ 77 Federal League

Newark's 1915 entry in the Federal League finished with a record of 80-72, good for fifth place in the eight-team circuit. The Peps, who played in hastily constructed Harrison Park, had a couple of premier players. One was outfielder Edd Roush, in his third year of pro ball and headed for the Hall of Fame. The other was pitcher Ed Reulbach, who posted a 20-10 won-lost record.

✿ 78 Dick Kazmaier

Princeton's perfect season in 1951 stemmed largely from senior quarterback Dick Kazmaier's brilliant performance. In the fifth game that year Kazmaier led the Tigers against previously unbeaten Cornell, scoring two touchdowns and passing for three more as Princeton overwhelmed the Big Red team, 53-15.

✿ 79 Goose Goslin

Outfielder Leon "Goose" Goslin (1900-71) spent 18 years in the majors with the Washington Senators, St. Louis Browns, and Detroit Tigers. His career stats earned him a Hall of Fame plaque in 1968, three years before his death. During his playing days, Goslin used to regale his friends in the off-season with baseball tales told on the veranda of Green's Hotel in Salem.

✿ 80 Mickey Walker

On November 1, 1922, the Toy Bulldog from Elizabeth won a furious 15-round bout at Madison Square Garden against Jack Britton to take the welterweight title. Four years later in Chicago he won the middleweight crown in a disputed decision against Tiger Flowers. Walker surrendered the title in 1931 without ever having defended it. Two years later he lost a light-heavyweight title match against Maxie Rosenbloom.

Answers ✿81 to ✿90 / Superlatives

✿ 81 Bill of Rights

After the passage of the U.S. Constitution, many Americans felt that certain additional safeguards were needed. The result was a

group of 12 proposed amendments, of which ten were passed—
the Bill of Rights. New Jersey ratified the Bill of Rights on
November 20, 1789, nearly a month before Maryland became the
second state to do so.

✿ 82   *The Star-Ledger*

For a long time it was called the *Newark Star-Ledger,* but with its
many regional editions and its widespread distribution in the
suburbs, it deleted the city's name. Nonetheless, its offices are at
Star-Ledger Plaza, Newark. Once regarded as second best to the
now-defunct *Newark News,* it has become New Jersey's largest
daily. Its circulation puts it 14th among American newspapers,
just below the *Philadelphia Inquirer.*

✿ 83   Hoboken

The fire started at about four in the afternoon among some
cotton stored on Pier 3. A strong wind caught the flames and
spread them to four nearby docked ships. One of them, the
Kaiser Wilhelm der Grosse, put to sea and suffered only minor
damage. The other three—the *Saale, Bremen,* and *Main*—burned,
with heavy loss of life: 326 people perished.

✿ 84   Rev. Hannibal Goodwin

In 1887 Rev. Hannibal Goodwin of Newark applied for a patent
on photographic film that could be wound on a spool. A delay in
granting the patent allowed a chemist at Eastman Kodak
Company to come up with the same idea. Kodak produced a
camera for the flexible film along with the film itself. Not until
1914 did Rev. Goodwin's widow win a judgment recognizing
Goodwin's prior claim.

✿ 85   Franklin

The New Jersey Zinc Company, with mines at Franklin and
nearby Ogdensburg, dominated the U.S. zinc industry for decades.
But even before zinc was extracted, the area was known for its
mining—mainly iron—and its startling variety of minerals, some of
them found no place else on earth. Many of the minerals remain,
but the mines are closed. Well, not completely. The Sterling
Mine in Ogdensburg recently reopened as a museum.

✿ 86 Bridgeton

First settled in 1686 when Richard Hancock built a sawmill, Bridgeton (for many years simply "The Bridge") became home in the early 1800s to a prosperous nail factory and a glassworks. Other glassmakers soon set themselves up in business. The nail factory closed in 1892. Various glassworks consolidated and in 1938 were bought out by Armstrong Cork Company. Food processing held sway for a time as the chief industry. Today Bridgeton's historic district attracts many visitors.

✿ 87 Elizabethtown

Elizabeth, once upon a time Elizabethtown, was settled in 1664. Since 1857 it has been the county seat of Union County. The 1664 date makes Elizabeth the oldest permanent European settlement in New Jersey, while the 1857 date makes Union the youngest established county. Elizabeth(town) and Newark were rivals for nearly 200 years, both of them major cities in Essex County. Finally, the people in Elizabeth had had enough. On March 18, 1857, they seceded, an act of disunion that prompted them, perversely, to name their new county Union. The two cities and counties went their separate but equally industrialized ways.

✿ 88 Round Valley Reservoir

Those who don't fish, and even those who do, may have difficulty with this one. Round Valley Reservoir is a sizable body of water by New Jersey standards, located south of I-78 between White House Station and Clinton. Not all of the Garden State's record fish are taken from large lakes, reservoirs, or rivers. The largest bluegill was taken from a Pennington farm pond, and a hefty 46½-pound carp was hauled from tiny Lake Parsippany.

✿ 89 William Franklin

Governor William Franklin, natural son of Benjamin Franklin, was arrested on the night of June 15, 1776, at the Proprietary House in Perth Amboy by Colonel Nathaniel Heard of the Continental army. William Franklin had moved there from his Green Bank estate in Burlington to try to head off the breaking of New Jersey's ties to the mother country. He failed. William Livingston replaced him as governor of the State of New Jersey.

✿ 90 Zarephath

Although there is a Zion in Somerset County, it does not have a post office or a ZIP Code. Zarephath, also in Somerset County, does. Southwest of Manville, the community was established by the Pillar of Fire, a religious sect founded by a Methodist minister's wife. A Christian radio station broadcasts from Zarephath.

Answers ✿91 to ✿100 / The Arts

✿ 91 *Cheaper by the Dozen*

Frank B. Gilbreth, Jr., and Ernestine Gilbreth Carey wrote this memoir, generally reviewed as "entertaining," "touching," and "hilarious," about their childhood in Montclair (although the story ranges at times from Nantucket to California). First published in 1948, it describes the goings-on in a 12-child household run as "a sort of school for scientific management and the elimination of wasted motions—or 'motion study,' as Dad and Mother called it."

✿ 92 Westfield

A "defrocked ghoul," Charles Addams cheerily called himself. His macabre cartoons amused *New Yorker* readers for five decades and led to a television series in the 1960s, "The Addams Family," and to a series of Addams Family movies. Charles Addams's father, a piano-company executive in Westfield, encouraged his son to draw. A typical result is the cartoon showing a grotesque-looking man outside a delivery room, with the nurse saying, "Congratulations, it's a baby."

✿ 93 Ben Shahn

Ben Shahn, born in Lithuania and raised in Brooklyn, made his art serve liberal social causes, starting in the Depression. He worked in a one-room studio behind his house in Jersey Homesteads (later Roosevelt), establishing his reputation in a style of art that some called poetic realism and others called social surrealism. From 1933 to 1938 he worked as a photographer for FDR's Farm Security Administration.

✿ 94 Crossroads Theatre Company
Located in the New Brunswick Cultural Center Complex, this acclaimed professional African-American theater company offers new plays, revivals, touring programs, and workshops. The theater was founded in 1978 by two Rutgers University students, Rick Khan and L. Kenneth Richardson.

✿ 95 Robert Louis Stevenson
While seeking an ideal climate for his tuberculosis, Robert Louis Stevenson (1850-94), the English author of *Treasure Island*, came to the United States, first to Saranac Lake, New York, then to Manasquan for a few weeks, before setting out for the South Seas. *The Master of Ballantrae* was published in 1889.

✿ 96 Spring Lake
The magnificent Essex-Sussex beach hotel was one of the many elegant buildings in Spring Lake during the seaside resort's golden era. Developed in the 1870s as a playground for the wealthy, this community, named for the small lake at its center, continues to exhibit some fine Victorian homes, hotels, and inns.

✿ 97 Montclair Art Museum
Founded in 1914, the Montclair Art Museum's pemanent collection includes significant works from the Hudson River School, American Impressionism, and the New York School of Abstract Expressionism. All of the art in the museum is American. Major artists such as George Innes (a Montclair resident), Edward Hopper, John Singer Sargent, and Willem de Kooning are represented. The museum, located at 3 South Mountain Avenue, also has a fine collection of Native American art and artifacts.

✿ 98 Alfred Stieglitz
Alfred Stieglitz (1864-1946) studied engineering in Berlin, but soon turned to photography, editing a series of photographic magazines. Beginning in 1905, his Manhattan gallery, "291," promoted photography as a fine art, and Stieglitz, whose own brilliant camera work helped to prove the point, raised the aesthetic status of photography considerably. He married Georgia O'Keeffe in 1924.

☆ 99 McCarter Theatre

Built as a permanent home for the Princeton University Triangle Club, it opened its doors in 1930 with a Triangle show, *The Golden Dog*. One of the stars was Josh Logan, a Princeton junior. Sophomore Jimmy Stewart sang in the chorus. Since that opening, McCarter has been the scene of many world premiers of Broadway shows, including, in 1938, Thornton Wilder's *Our Town*. A number of stars have gotten their start on the McCarter stage, including John Lithgow and Christopher Reeve.

☆ 100 Dorothy Kirsten

Operatic soprano Dorothy Kirsten enriched the world of opera for more than 40 years. She made her debut in Chicago in 1940 and at the Met in 1945. A year later she appeared as a popular diva on the cover of *Life* magazine. Kirsten made several recordings, some of them of light opera and popular songs. She was often paired with Gordon MacRae, a native of East Orange. She even made a record with Bing Crosby. Her autobiography, *A Time to Sing*, was published in 1982.

Answers to Bonus Puzzlers 9 to 12

9 / A Few Forgettable Films **a.** The Toxic Avenger (sometimes referred to as "Toxie") **b.** *Superman* **c.** *Friday the 13th* **d.** *New Jersey Drive* **e.** *King of the Gypsies*

10 / From Jersey to Stardom **a.** Michael Douglas **b.** Ice-T **c.** Andrew Shue **d.** Danny DeVito **e.** David Copperfield

11 / Who's the Governor? **a.** Alfred E. Driscoll **b.** William Paterson **c.** Walter E. Edge **d.** Charles Edison e. Brendan Byrne

12 / Monumental Events **a.** Battle of Princeton **b.** Peter Stuyvesant **c.** Carranza, a pilot, crashed after returning a good-will flight that Charles A. Lindbergh had made to Mexico. **d.** First African-American voter after ratification of 15th Amendment **e.** Peter J. McGuire

Answers to Bonus Puzzlers 13 to 16

13 / A QUINTET OF COURTHOUSES **a.** Essex **b.** Hunterdon
c. Burlington **d.** Middlesex **e.** Camden

14 / HERE, THERE, AND ALL OVER Possible answers: **a.** Berlin
Bogota, Hamburg, Stockholm, Vienna **b.** Austria,
Switzerland, Denmark, Finland, Norway, Lithuania,
Ireland, Albania, and others **c.** Dover, Englewood,
Jersey City, Lambertville, Montclair, Mountain Lakes,
and others **d.** Belvidere, Cape May Court House,
Flemington, Mays Landing, Newton, Salem,
Toms River **e.** Keyport, Oceanport, Port Elizabeth, Port
Monmouth, Port Norris, Port Republic, and others

15 / OH, ALMA MATER **a.** Fairleigh Dickinson/Teaneck-
Hackensack **b.** William Paterson **c.** Seton Hall
d. Jersey City State **e.** Lions

16 / THE LAST NAME'S THE SAME **a.** Gibson **b.** Dodge **c.** Stevens
d. Dee **e.** O'Hara

The Author

Gerald Tomlinson is the author of
Murdered in Jersey and co-author
with Ronald A. Mayer of *The New
Jersey Book of Lists.* Several of
his short stories have appeared in
Ellery Queen's Mystery Magazine
and in various anthologies. For a
number of years he was an editor
in trade and textbook publishing.
With his wife, Alexis, he has lived
in Fort Lee, Parsippany, and for
the past 25 years in Lake Hopatcong.